Salary Negotiation
Tips for Professionals

By Ron and Caryl Krannich

CAREER AND BUSINESS BOOKS AND SOFTWARE

101 Dynamite Answers to Interview Questions
101 Secrets of Highly Effective Speakers
201 Dynamite Job Search Letters
America's Top 100 Jobs for People Without a Four-Year Degree
America's Top Jobs for People Re-Entering the Workforce
America's Top Internet Job Sites
Best Jobs for the 21st Century
Change Your Job, Change Your Life
The Complete Guide to Public Employment
The Directory of Federal Jobs and Employers
Discover the Best Jobs for You!
Dynamite Cover Letters
Dynamite Resumes
Dynamite Salary Negotiations
Dynamite Tele-Search
The Educator's Guide to Alternative Jobs and Careers
Find a Federal Job Fast!
From Air Force Blue to Corporate Gray
From Army Green to Corporate Gray
From Navy Blue to Corporate Gray
Get a Raise in 7 Days
High Impact Resumes and Letters
I Want to Do Something Else, But I'm Not Sure What It Is
Interview for Success
The Job Hunting Guide: Transitioning From College to Career
Job Hunting Tips for People With Not-So-Hot Backgrounds
Job Interview Tips for People With Not-So-Hot Backgrounds
Job-Power Source and Ultimate Job Source (software)
Jobs and Careers With Nonprofit Organizations
Military Resumes and Cover Letters
Moving Out of Education
Moving Out of Government
Nail the Job Interview!
No One Will Hire Me!
Re-Careering in Turbulent Times
Salary Negotiation Tips for Professionals
Savvy Interviewing
Savvy Networker
Savvy Resume Writer

TRAVEL AND INTERNATIONAL BOOKS

Best Resumes and CVs for International Jobs
The Complete Guide to International Jobs and Careers
The Directory of Websites for International Jobs
International Jobs Directory
Jobs for Travel Lovers
Politics of Family Planning Policy in Thailand
Shopping and Traveling in Exotic Asia
Shopping in Exotic Places
Shopping the Exotic South Pacific
Travel Planning On the Internet
Treasures and Pleasures of Australia
Treasures and Pleasures of Bermuda
Treasures and Pleasures of China
Treasures and Pleasures of Egypt
Treasures and Pleasures of Hong Kong
Treasures and Pleasures of India
Treasures and Pleasures of Indonesia
Treasures and Pleasures of Italy
Treasures and Pleasures of Mexico
Treasures and Pleasures of Paris
Treasures and Pleasures of Rio and São Paulo
Treasures and Pleasures of Santa Fe, Taos, and Albuquerque
Treasures and Pleasures of Singapore and Bali
Treasures and Pleasures of Singapore and Malaysia
Treasures and Pleasures of South America
Treasures and Pleasures of Southern Africa
Treasures and Pleasures of Thailand and Myanmar
Treasures and Pleasures of Turkey
Treasures and Pleasures of Vietnam and Cambodia

Salary Negotiation Tips for Professionals

Compensation That Reflects Your Value

Ron and Caryl Krannich, Ph.Ds

IMPACT PUBLICATIONS
Manassas Park, VA

Salary Negotiation Tips for Professionals

ISBN: 1-57023-230-X

Library of Congress: 2004112117

Publisher: For information on Impact Publications, including current and forthcoming publications, authors, press kits, online bookstore, and submission requirements, visit the left navigation bar on the front page of our main company website: www.impactpublications.com.

Publicity/Rights: For information on publicity, author interviews, and subsidiary rights, contact the Media Relations Department: Tel. 703-361-7300, Fax 703-335-9486, or email: info@impactpublications.com.

Sales/Distribution: All bookstore sales are handled through Impact's trade distributor: National Book Network, 15200 NBN Way, Blue Ridge Summit, PA 17214, Tel. 1-800-462-6420. All special sales and distribution inquiries should be directed to the publisher: Sales Department, IMPACT PUBLICATIONS, 9104 Manassas Drive, Suite N, Manassas Park, VA 20111-5211, Tel. 703-361-7300, Fax 703-335-9486, or email: info@impactpublications.com.

Contents

Preface

WELCOME TO THE FIRST volume in our new "The 75,000+ Job Search Series." Designed for professionals seeking jobs that pay in excess of $75,000 a year, books in this series quickly prepare such individuals for major steps in the job search process. Based on the experiences of seasoned career experts and executive-level job seekers, these books provide inside tips on how to best land a job, from writing resumes and cover letters to networking, interviewing, and negotiating terms of employment.

We're pleased that you are joining us on what may well become one of the most exciting journeys, and defining moments, in your career and your life – finalizing a job offer by negotiating an excellent compensation package that truly reflects your talents. As many employers often discover too late, if money doesn't talk, talent walks. And as many employees well know, the salary they initially negotiate with an employer affects their compensation for many years to come. Therefore, it is important that you do this right from the very start as well as negotiate the best salary possible at every stage of your work life. As you will quickly discover, the whole, usually reticent, process of talking money to power can be extremely rewarding if you know how to approach this process properly. Indeed, if you put this book into practice, it should be worth thousands of dollars in additional compensation today and in the future. It may well be one of the most financially rewarding books you will ever read and put into use.

Be forewarned that this is not your typical job search book. Researched and client-based, it represents the collective efforts of hundreds of career professionals who have worked with thousands of clients over the past five decades in preparing them for the critical salary negotiation session. Indeed, during the past six years, we have had the opportunity to work closely with a group of dedicated career professionals (Career Advisors associated with Bernard Haldane Associates) who have counseled thousands of job seekers on how to best negotiate salary and terms of employment. Given our unique access to their client files and personnel, we have been able to examine and analyze some of the most revealing stories of salary success. Dealing with real cases of success from the job search trenches, we outline what does and does not work in the $75,000+ job world. Experienced in the day-to-day realities of finding jobs and changing careers, many of these professionals represent the cutting edge of career management. Indeed, they have pioneered many innovative assessment, networking, interviewing, and salary negotiating techniques that are now standard practices among career professionals and job seekers.

> *As many employers often discover too late, if money doesn't talk, talent walks.*

If you follow the advice outlined in this book, you should do very well in negotiating an excellent compensation package that truly reflects what you have achieved and will do in the future for your employer. You will be in a powerful position to negotiate a well-deserved compensation package, because you incorporated several effective salary negotiation tips and techniques used daily by thousands of clients and which are outlined in this book:

- value a position and themselves
- listen more than talk
- postpone salary discussion
- persuade the employer to show his hand first
- respond to an offer with a 30-second pause

- focus on the total picture
- choose battles carefully
- consider incentivized pay and renegotiation options
- request time to consider an offer

Best of all, as a professional always negotiating in a professional manner, you will incorporate tips and techniques that will help you develop a very positive and productive relationship with your new employer who believes he or she made the right hiring decision.

We wish you well as you face this final phase of your job search – negotiating terms of employment. If you follow the experiences, principles, strategies, and tips outlined in this book, you should be able to achieve your salary goals as well as develop a positive and productive relationship with your new employer.

Ron and Caryl Krannich
krannich@impactpublications.com

Salary Negotiation Tips for Professionals

1

Making More Money Through Negotiations

HAT ARE YOU REALLY worth in today's job market? Are you prepared to talk money to power (a prospective employer or your boss)? Can you effectively negotiate a salary that is 25 percent higher than your last salary? Do you know what should be included in a compensation package and how much it should be worth in reference to your base salary? Are you prepared to negotiate stock options, a signing bonus, equity pay, vacation time, and a golden parachute? Does your resume, interview answers, and success stories stress a pattern of accomplishments, as well as help predict your future performance with a new employer? Can you justify what you believe you're really worth?

Skills for Getting What You're Worth

Not surprising, most people think they are worth more than what's reflected in their current paycheck. While they may feel underpaid, few of them are prepared to do much about it. When, for example, was the last time you approached your boss for a raise . . . and got it? When was the last time you quit your job and found one that paid what you felt you were really worth? And when was the last time you

1

confidently went into a salary negotiation session and came out with exactly what you wanted? If you are like most job seekers, you could use some sound advice on improving your salary negotiation skills.

That's our goal in the following pages – equip you with the necessary knowledge and skills to get what you're really worth in today's job market. If you follow many of our negotiation tips, you should be able to effectively negotiate your next compensation package and substantially increase your income. Using our techniques, many job seekers are able to negotiate a salary 10 to 20 percent higher than initially offered by an employer. Since your most recent salary affects your subsequent salaries, how well you negotiate your salary can mean thousands of dollars in additional income over the next 10 years.

It's About Your Talent for Money

Let's start by simplifying rather than complicating the salary negotiation process by focusing on the basics of employment relationships. Work means many things to different people. But the bottom line is money – it's all about valuing your talent, positions, and work and then translating those values into various forms of compensation, be it cash, equity shares, or benefits. The value of jobs can be translated into specific dollar amounts for determining compensation – $50,000, $100,000, $250,000, or more. It's your talent in exchange for position and compensation. After all, you have expenses and a lifestyle that require a regular paycheck. If you forget this basic money concept of work, you may place yourself at a major disadvantage in today's workplace. Like many people, you may find yourself under-compensated for your level of responsibilities and talent. If you merely accept what an employer initially offers, without weighing it against market values, you may later become unhappy with your job when you learn you are under-compensated compared to others with similar experience and talent.

The bottom line for work is money – your talent in exchange for position and compensation.

Clients of our associates know their value when it comes time to negotiate a compensation package. Before going to a job interview, they do their research in preparation for negotiating in a positive, proactive, and professional manner. They know what added value they will bring to the workplace, and they clearly communicate that value to potential employers who understand the economics of hiring the right talent. Most important of all, they know how to talk money to power – one of the more important and rewarding skills you must learn in conducting an effective job search. They invariably end up in jobs that pay more than their last job. Their success is usually a direct function of practicing the many salary negotiation techniques and tips outlined in this book.

Finding Your Right "Fit"

Anyone can find a job, but finding the right job – one you do well and truly enjoy doing – is the most challenging task for most job seekers. It's not enough to just write a resume and send it to employers in response to job vacancies. Finding a quality job, one that is right for you, involves assessing your skills, developing a clear objective, researching employ-ment options, and targeting specific employers. In other volumes we've

> _Your goal should be to find a job that is a perfect "fit" for your particular pattern of accomplishments._

outlined critical communication skills which are based upon proven principles of effective career management developed by the father of modern career counseling, Dr. Bernard Haldane: _Haldane's Best Resumes for Professionals_, _Haldane's Best Cover Letters for Profession-als_, _Haldane's Best Answers to Tough Interview Questions_, and _Change Your Job, Change Your Life_. Each of these volumes is based upon a clear set of principles, honed over more than 50 years of experience in working with hundreds of thousands of job seekers who have paid substantial career counseling and coaching fees for such insider advice. These principles are designed to ensure that they find the best possible "fit" in today's job market. By "fit" we mean aligning one's interests, skills, abilities, and goals with jobs that require such characteristics. Your goal should be to find a job that is a perfect "fit" for your particular pattern of accomplishments. Once you recognize your pattern and align it with a job you know that you will do well and enjoy doing, your value to employers should be considerable. You should be in a position to negotiate an attractive compensation package, because both you and the employer know you will bring special value to the position and the company.

Talking Money to Strangers

When was the last time you talked about other people's salaries? Have you ever walked up to someone and asked how much they made?

Given the secretive nature of salary information, many people are "salary dumb" when it comes time to talk money to power.

Alternatively, what would you say if someone walked up to you and asked *"How much do you make?"* Chances are you would not be very forthcoming with an answer to what many people feel is a relatively shocking or rude question. Your salary is your business – a secret between you, your employer, and perhaps close relatives – and other people's salaries are their business. After all, our culture teaches us that it's not nice to ask people what they make. Given the secretive nature of salary information, many people are relatively "salary dumb" when it comes time to talk about money to important strangers – employers. Not knowing what others make, most job seekers go into the job interview naive about money and other forms of compensation. Many candidates accept what the employer initially offers as the appropriate salary for the position and their talent. And those who do negotiate their salary often make numerous mistakes that can lead to on-the-job complications once they accept a job offer.

Learning and Communicating Value

As outlined in our companion volumes – *Haldane's Best Answers to Tough Interview Questions, Dynamic Salary Negotiations, Get a Raise in 7 Days, Interview for Success,* and *Nail the Job Interview* – much of your job search should focus on learning about the value of positions as well as communicating your value to potential employers. Indeed, the whole job interview process should be a two-way communication process: you want to learn as much as possible about the position and employer in order to **value the job**, and the employer should learn as much as possible about your potential value to the organization in order to **value your talents**. While you come at it from different perspectives, you're both talking about money and how it should be best assigned to you and the position. The interview should never involve clever "gotcha" negotiation strategies which often border on the unethical – lying or exaggerating one's salary history, alternative job offers, and performance capabilities. Nor do you want employers exaggerating company benefits or making compensation and advancement promises they cannot keep. To do so would invariably set the wrong tone for your future relationship with the employer.

What Employers Want From You

You should always focus on communicating your **accomplishments** to prospective employers. For it's those accomplishments that bring value to both you and the position. From the perspective of employers, your past pattern of accomplishments translates into potential benefits for the company – the outcomes for which you

As a productive, employer-centered professional, you need to speak both truth and money to power.

will be compensated and held accountable. Many employers are more than willing to provide average or above market compensation, including creative compensation schemes, to acquire such benefits.

Focusing on employers' bottom lines – what they really value the most in their employees – your job is to convince employers that you will bring X amount of **benefits** to the organization. Accordingly, as an untested employee in a new organization, you want to be initially compensated to a level that reflects your potential productivity as indicated from your past pattern of productivity. As a productive, employer-centered professional, you need to speak both truth and money to power. The salary negotiation techniques you employ should focus on translating your value into benefits for the employer and company. Always stay focused on what's most important to you and the employer – your value, benefits, productivity, and accomplishments. Again, staying focused means you want to talk about those things that are important to both you and the employer – your talent and projected future performance in exchange for compensation in the form of cash and benefits.

Working With a Career Professional

While the information in this book will help you negotiate a compensation package on your own, at the same time, you may want use the services of a seasoned career professional. Anyone can conduct a job search on their own and find a job. But we assume you don't want to find just any job. You want a high quality job that is the right fit for both you and the employer – one you really enjoy doing and one that benefits both you and the employer.

Client Feedback

"Right from the beginning, your techniques helped build my self esteem, gave me direction, and helped me increase my salary 100% more than my previous position with less frustration and stress than before."
– M.H.

Unfortunately, the novice do-it-yourself approach often results in taking shortcuts rather than doing first things first. For example, most job seekers begin their job search by first writing their resume rather than doing the necessary foundation work that should be the basis for their resume and other key job search activities, such as networking, interviewing, and negotiating. After all, they say, isn't that what you're supposed to do first, because that's what others always do? Some, as indicated by the popularity of resume example books, even go so far as to creatively plagiarize others' resumes. By following the crowd, they literally put the horse before the cart and thereby immediately handicap their job search with an ill-fitting resume that may communicate all the wrong messages!

You owe it to yourself to present your very best self to employers. That means taking the time and spending some money to do first things first when conducting a job search. The prerequisite foundation work involves self-assessment and goal setting – two activities that may be best done with the assistance of a career professional. If you fail to do this foundation work and go directly to writing your resume and interviewing for jobs, you will most likely join thousands of other do-it-yourself job seekers who meander through the job market trying to find a job they can fit into. You will find a job but chances are it will not be a good fit. You may be well advised to work with a career professional to identify what it is you do well and enjoy doing.

Shopping for Alternative Career Services

At least 12 different types of career planning and employment services are available to assist you with different phases of your job search, including salary negotiations. Each of these services has certain advantages and disadvantages. Approach them with caution as you shop around for the best services to meet your specific needs. Always remember that career planning is a big and relatively unregulated business where you will occasionally encounter hucksters and fraudulent services aimed at taking advantage of individuals who are psychologically vulnerable and naive. Many of these hucksters self-certify themselves, engage in questionable screening practices, promise to locate jobs that pay more than your last one, and seal the deal by asking for up-front money – $500 to $15,000 – to find you a job. Lacking good shopping sense and engaging in wishful thinking, many job seekers fall for the false promises of these so-called employment experts.

Our advice is very simple: Never sign a contract before you read the fine print, get a second opinion, and talk to former clients about the **results** they achieved through the service. While most of these services are not free, there is no reason to believe that the most expensive services are the best services. In fact, you may get the same quality of services from a group that charges $300 versus one that costs $15,000. At the same time, free or cheap services are not necessarily as good as the more expensive services. While you often get what you pay for in this industry, you also may get much less than what you pay for. Again, before using any employment services or hiring an expert, do your research by contacting a few individuals who have used the services.

With these words of caution in mind, let's examine a variety of services available, which you may or may not want to incorporate in your career planning and job search efforts.

1. Public employment services

Public employment services usually consist of a state agency which provides employment assistance as well as dispenses unemployment compensation benefits. Employment assistance largely consists of job listings and counseling services. However, counseling services often screen individuals for employers who list with the public employment agency. If you are looking for an entry-level job or a job paying $18,000 to $40,000, contact these services. Most employers still do not list with them, especially for positions paying more than $40,000 a year. Although the main purpose of these offices has been to dispense unemployment benefits, don't overlook them because of past stereotypes. The Workforce Development Act has re-energized such services. Within the past four years, many of these offices have literally "reinvented" themselves for today's new job market with One-Stop Career Centers, computerized job banks, counseling services, training programs, and other innovative organizational and technical approaches. Many of them offer useful employment services, including self-assessment and job search workshops as well as access to job listings on the Internet. Most of these offices are linked to America's Job Bank (www.ajb.dni.us), an electronic job bank which includes over 1 million job listings throughout the U.S. and abroad. This is one of the premier employment websites that offers a wealth of information and resources for job seekers. It's one all job seekers need to become familiar with. America's Job Bank, in turn, is linked to the U.S. Department of Labor's three other useful websites – America's CareerInfoNet (www.acinet.org), America's Service Locator (www.servicelocator.org), and Career OneStop (www.careeronestop.org). If you are a veteran, you will find many of the jobs listed with state employment offices give veterans preference in hiring. These centers should be able to give you information on salary ranges for various positions in your community – important information you need. Many of these centers increasingly work with professionals earning more than $50,000 a year.

2. Private employment agencies

Private employment agencies work for money, either from applicants or employers. Approximately 8,000 such agencies operate nationwide. Many are highly specialized in technical, scientific, and financial fields. The majority of these firms serve the interests of employers, since employers – not applicants – represent repeat business. While employers normally pay the placement fee, many agencies charge applicants 10 to 15 percent of their first year salary. These firms have one major advantage: job leads which you may have difficulty uncovering elsewhere. Especially for highly specialized fields, a good firm can be extremely helpful. The major disadvantages are that they can be costly and the quality of the firms varies. Be careful in how you deal with them. Make sure you understand the fee structure and what they will do for you before you sign anything. The bi-annual directory *JobBank Guide to Employment Services* (Adams Media) includes data on nearly 3,000 firms.

3. Temporary staffing firms

During the past decade temporary staffing firms have come of age as more and more employers turn to them for recruitment assistance. They offer a variety of employment services to both applicants and employers who are either looking for temporary work and workers or who want to better screen applicants and employers. Many of these firms, such as Manpower (www.man power.com), Olsten (www.olsten.com), and Kelly Services (www.kellyservices.com), recruit individuals for a wide range of positions and skill levels as well as full-time employment. Some firms, such as Robert Half International (www.rhii.com) specialize in certain types of workers (accounting, law, information technology, or computer personnel). If you are interested in "testing the job waters," you may want to contact these firms for information on their services. Employers – not job seekers – pay for these services. While many of these firms are listed in the Yellow Pages, most have websites. The following websites are especially popular with individuals interested in part-time

or contract work: www.net-temps.com, www.elance.com, www.
ework.com, www.guru.com, www.contractorforum.com, and
http://ct.monster.com.

4. College/university placement offices

College and university placement offices provide in-house career
planning services for graduating students. While some give
assistance to alumni, don't expect too much help if you have
already graduated; you may, instead, need to contact the alumni
office which may offer employment services. Many college
placement offices are understaffed or provide only rudimentary
services, such as maintaining a career planning library, coordi-
nating on-campus interviews for graduating seniors, and
conducting workshops on how to write resumes and interview.
Others provide a full range of well supported services including
testing and one-on-one counseling. Indeed, many community
colleges offer such services to members of the community on a
walk-in basis. You can use their libraries and computerized
career assessment programs, take personality and interest inven-
tories, or attend special workshops or full-semester career
planning courses which will take you through each step of the
career planning and job search processes. You may want to
enroll in such a course since it is likely to provide just enough
structure and content to assess your motivated abilities and
skills and to assist you in implementing a successful job search
plan. Check with your local campus to see what services you
might use. Many of the college and university placement offices
belong to the National Association of Colleges and Employers,
which operates its own employment website: www.jobweb.com.
This site includes a wealth of information on employment for
college graduates (see the "Site Map" section: www.jobweb.
com/search/sitemap.htm). Its "Career Library" section includes
direct links to hundreds of college and university placement
offices: www.jobweb.com/Career-Development/collegeres.htm.
To find college alumni offices, visit the following websites:
www.alumni.net, www.bcharrispub.com, and www.jobweb.com/
After_College. Since colleges and universities tend to be very

web-savvy, you can visit hundreds of their career websites to acquire all types of useful free information on conducting an effective job search. One of our favorites is the website operated by the Career Center at the College of William and Mary (www. wm.edu/career). Indeed, searching many of these college and university websites is comparable to having your own personal career counselor – without having to go to college!

5. Private career and job search firms

Private career and job search firms help individuals acquire job search skills and coach them through the process of finding a job. They do not find you a job. In other words, they teach you much of what is outlined in this book. Expect to pay anywhere from $1,500 to $10,000 for this service. If you need a structured environment for conducting your job search, contract with one of these firms for professional assistance. One of the major such firms used to be Bernard Haldane Associates (they ceased operating under that name and became BH Careers International, www.bhcareers.com, in 2004). Many of their pioneering career planning and job search methods are incorporated in this book as well as can be found in five other key job search books: *Haldane's Best Resumes for Professionals, Haldane's Best Cover Letters for Professionals, Haldane's Best Answers to Tough Interview Questions, Haldane's Best Salary Tips for Professionals*, and *Haldane's Best Employment Websites for Professionals* (Impact Publications – see the order form at the end of this book or www.impactpublications.com). Other firms offering similar services include Right Management Consultants (www. right.com), R. L. Stevens & Associates (www.interviewing.com), and Lee Hecht Harrison (www.lhh.com/us).

6. Executive search firms and headhunters

Executive search firms work for employers in finding employees to fill critical positions in the $50,000 plus salary range. They also are called "headhunters," "management consultants," and "executive recruiters." These firms play an important role in linking high level technical and managerial talent to organizations. Don't expect to contract for these services. Executive recruiters work for employers, not applicants. If a friend or relative is in this business or you have relevant skills of interest to these firms, let them know you are available – and ask for their advice. On the other hand, you may want to contact firms that specialize in recruiting individuals with your skill specialty. For a comprehensive listing of these firms, see the latest annual edition of *The Directory of Executive Recruiters* (Kennedy Information, www.kennedyinfo.com; also see the order form at the end of this book and www.impactpublications.com). Several companies, such as www.resumezapper.com, www.blastmyresu me.com, and www.resumeblaster.com, offer e-mail resume blasting services that primarily target headhunters. For a fee, which usually ranges from $50 to $200, these firms will blast your resume to 5,000 to 10,000 headhunters. This is a quick, easy, and inexpensive way to reach thousands of headhunters and executive search firms. This resume distribution method also may be a waste of time and money. Approach it with a sense of healthy skepticism.

7. Marketing services

Marketing services represent an interesting combination of job search and executive search activities. They can cost $2,500 or more, and they work with individuals anticipating a starting salary of at least $75,000 but preferably over $100,000. These firms try to minimize the time and risk of applying for jobs. A typical operation begins with a client paying a $150 fee for developing psychological, skills, and interests profiles. If you pass this stage – most anyone with money does – you go on to the next one-on-one stage. At this point, a marketing plan is outlined and a contract signed for specific services. Work for the clients usually involves activities centered on the resume and interviewing. Using word processing software, the firm normally develops a slick "professional" resume and sends it by mail or e-mail, along with a cover letter, to hundreds – maybe thousands – of firms. Clients are then briefed and sent to interview with interested employers. While you can save money and achieve the same results on your own, these firms do have one major advantage: They save you **time** by doing most of the work for you. Again, approach these services with caution and with the knowledge that you can probably do just as well – if not better – on your own by following the step-by-step advice of many job search books.

8. Women's centers and special career services

Women's centers and special career services for displaced workers, such as 40-Plus Clubs (www.40plus.org/chapters) and Five O'Clock Clubs (www.fiveoclockclub.com), have been established to respond to the employment needs of special groups. Women's centers are particularly active in sponsoring career planning workshops and job information networks. These centers tend to be geared toward elementary job search activities, because many of their clientele consist of homemakers who are entering or re-entering the workforce with little knowledge of the job market. Special career services arise at times for different categories of employees. For example, unemployed aerospace engineers, teachers, veterans, air traffic controllers, and government employees have formed special groups for developing job search skills and sharing job leads.

9. Testing and assessment centers

Testing and assessment centers provide assistance for identifying vocational skills, interests, and objectives. Usually staffed by trained professionals, these centers administer several types of tests and charge from $200 to $900 per person. If you use such services, make sure you are given one or both of the two most popular and reliable tests: *Myers-Briggs Type Indicator®* and the *Strong Interest Inventory®*. You should find both tests helpful in better understanding your interests and decision-making styles. In many cases, the career office at your local community college or women's center can administer these tests at minimum cost ($20 to $40). At the same time, many of these testing and assessment services are now available online. Check out these popular websites: www.skillsone.com, www.self-directed-search. com, www.careerlab.com, www.personalityonline.com, www.as sessment.com, and www.personalitytype.com. An alternative set of tests and assessment activities can be found in our book, *I Want to Do Something Else, But I'm Not Sure What It Is* (Impact Publications, 2005).

10. Job fairs and career conferences

Job fairs and career conferences are organized by a variety of groups – from schools and government agencies to headhunters, employment agencies, and professional associations – to link applicants to employers. **Job fairs** are often open to the public and involve many employers. **Career conferences** may be closed to the public (invitation only) and involve a single employer. Usually consisting of one- to two-day meetings in a hotel or conference center, employers meet with applicants as a group and on a one-to-one basis. Employers give presentations on their companies, applicants circulate resumes, and employers interview candidates. Many such conferences are organized to attract hard-to-recruit groups, such as engineers, computer programmers, individuals with security clearances, and clerical and service workers, or for special population groups, such as minorities, transitioning military personnel, women, people with disabilities, and even ex-offenders. These are excellent sources for job leads and information on specific employers and jobs – if you are invited to attend or if the meeting is open to the public. Employers pay for this service, although some job fairs and career conferences may charge job seekers a nominal regis- tration fee.

11. Professional associations

Professional associations often provide placement assistance. This usually consists of listing job vacancies in publications, maintaining a resume database, and organizing a job informa- tion exchange at annual conferences. Some may even organize job fairs, such as the Military Officers Association (www.moaa. org) and the Non-Commissioned Officers Association (www. ncoausa.org). Many large associations operate their own online employment sites; members can include their resume in an electronic database and employers can access the database to search for qualified candidates. Annual conferences are good sources for making job contacts in different geographic locations within a particular professional field. But don't expect too much. Talking to people (networking) at professional conferences may yield better results than reading job listings, placing your resume online, or interviewing at conference placement centers. For excellent online directories of professional associations, be sure to visit these two sites: www.ipl.org/ref/AON and www.asaenet.org.

12. Professional resume writers

Professional resume writers are increasingly playing an important role in career planning. Each year thousands of job seekers rely on these professionals for assistance in writing their resumes. Many of these professionals also provide useful job search tips on resume distribution, cover letters, and networking as well as include other career planning and job search services, such as assessment, mentoring, and practice interviewing. Charging from $100 to $600 for writing a resume, they work with the whole spectrum of job seekers – entry-level to senior executives making millions of dollars each year. While some are certified career counselors, many of these professionals have their own associations and certification groups that include a large assortment of often unintelligible initials after their names – CAC, CBC, CCM, CEIP, CHRE, CIPC, CPC, CPRW, JCTC, LPC, NBCC, NCC, NCCC, NCRW, and PCC. If you are interested in working with a professional resume writer, visit the following websites for information on this network of career professionals: www.parw.com, www.prwra.com, www.cminsti tute.com, and www.nrwaweb.com. Examples of their high-end work can be found in Wendy Enelow's two books: *Best Resumes for $100,000+ Jobs* and *Best Cover Letters for $100,000+ Jobs*

(Impact Publications – see order form at the end of this book or visit the publisher's online bookstore: www.impactpublications. com).

Finding Certified Career Professionals

Certified career professionals are experienced in working one-on-one with clients, with special emphasis on career assessment. They have their own professional associations. If you are interested in contacting a certified career professional for assistance, we advise you to first visit these websites for locating a career professional:

- **National Board for Certified Counselors, Inc.**   www.nbcc.org
- **National Career Development Association**   www.ncda.org
- **Certified Career Coaches**   www.certifiedcareer coaches.com
- **Career Planning and Adult Development Network**   www.careernetwork.org

You also can find a great deal of professional career assistance through the U.S. Department of Labor's website, which enables users to locate services within their communities:

- **America's Service Locator**   www.servicelocator.org

On Your Own or With a Little Help

Other types of career planning and employment services are growing and specializing in particular occupational fields. You may wish to use these services as a supplement to this book.

Whatever you do, be a smart shopper for career planning and job search services. Proceed with caution, know exactly what you are getting into, and choose the best. Remember, there is no such thing as a free lunch, and you often get less than what you pay for. At the same time, the most expensive services are not necessarily the best. Indeed, the free and inexpensive career planning services offered by many community or junior colleges – libraries, computerized career assessment programs, testing, and workshops – may be all you need. On the other hand, don't be afraid to spend some money on getting the best services. You may quickly discover that this money was well spent when you land a job that pays 20 to 40 percent more than your previous job! Whatever you do, don't be *"pennywise but pound foolish"* by trying to do your job search on the cheap. If you have difficulty writing a first-class resume, by all means contact a resume-writing pro who can put together a dynamite resume that truly represents what you have done, can do, and will do in the future.

After reading this book, you should be able to make intelligent decisions about what, when, where, and with what results you can use professional assistance. Shop around, compare services and costs, ask questions, talk to former clients, and read the fine print before giving an employment expert a job using your hard earned money. Don't try to be the Lone Ranger all of the time. If necessary, contact a career professional at different stages of your job search. A career expert could very well become your best friend in the process of finding employment that's right for you.

Don't try to be the Lone Ranger all of the time. If necessary, contact a career professional at different stages of your job search.

Indeed, let's talk truth about what we're dealing with in the world of self-help and enlightenment. It can be very lonely and depressing out there in the job market. Our experience, as well as that of most career professionals, is that very few individuals conduct the job search process well on their own. Not that they can't; it's just that they won't and thus they don't. Understanding, yes; action, some, but not enough sustained, purposeful action to make things happen the way they should. Most job seekers can cognitively understand what's involved in conducting a successful job search, such as networking, but the actual process of putting it all together, finding time, implementing each step properly, remaining focused, and maintaining a high level of motivation and energy in the face of no responses or ego-wrenching rejections is something that is very difficult to do on their own. Not surprisingly, people normally used to being effective all of a sudden feel ineffective when conducting their own job search. Nothing seems to work according to expectation, or perhaps expectations are either too high or misplaced. They procrastinate, find excuses, get depressed, and give up in what is often a cycle of good intentions and dashed expectations with sustained action conspicuously absent. Indeed, very few people ever do it right on their own. Accordingly, most people can benefit tremendously by using the services of a career expert. A career management professional can save you a great deal of time, money, and headaches, because they combine expertise with a structure for implementing a job search campaign. This expertise comes in many forms:

- testing and assessing
- developing and targeting a job search plan
- assisting with writing resumes and letters
- honing networking skills
- implementing an action plan
- coaching for job interviews and salary negotiations

Most important of all, a professional can serve as both a coach and mentor who helps you maintain your focus and motivation as well as provides a critical structure for routinely implementing each phase of your job search.

It's Also More Than Just Money

Whether you choose to do your job search on your own or with the assistance of a career professional, the important thing to remember is that you are dealing with money – your talent in exchange for the employer's compensation package. Don't short-change yourself by failing to approach this process in the best and most professional manner possible. If you are not used to talking money to power, then it's time to get prepared to do so with the help of this book and other resources. You may well discover a few basic negotiating techniques, such as the pregnant 30-second pause, which may result in $5,000 to $10,000 in additional compensation. Also, remember to always negotiate in a very professional manner – no tricks, no lies, no hype. Just the full truth about your talent and value in exchange for the best compensation package possible. For in the end, how you negotiate your salary also may determine how well you do on the job.

Coming Up

The following chapters reveal numerous salary negotiation tips that individuals who earn in excess of $50,000 a year have used to negotiate compensation packages that reflect their true value. We begin in Chapter 2, **"Common Mistakes You Must Avoid,"** by reviewing many common blunders job seekers make when negotiating as well as outlining key skills of savvy salary negotiators. Chapter 3, **"Major Compensation Options and Issues,"** reviews various compensation alternatives that you should consider before entering into a salary negotiation session. Chapter 4, **"Calculate Your Worth,"** offers numerous tips on how you can best figure how much you are really worth in today's job market. Chapter 5, **"Deal Effectively With Compensation Issues,"** outlines key compensation issues you need to handle in any salary negotiation, with special reference to keeping focused on what's really important to you and the employer. Chapter 6, **"Asking and Answering Salary Questions,"** addresses common situations in which you are requested to provide a salary history or salary requirements; it offers tips on how to deal with questions that may prematurely reveal your hand and thus put you at a disadvantage. Chapter 7, **"Negotiate a Winning Compensation Package,"** takes you through the process of negotiating compensation, from whom should initiate the subject to actually signing a compensation agreement. Chapter 8, **"Getting Raises and Promotions,"** offers numerous tips on addressing compensation issues once on the job in the form of raises and promotions. Chapter 9, **"The Quick and Easy Salary Advisor,"** includes dozens of questions and corresponding answers relating to some of the most important compensation issues facing job seekers.

We wish you well in your job search. If you put into practice several of the salary negotiation tips identified in this book, you should be able to negotiate your next compensation package with confidence and the knowledge that you have done your very best in getting top dollar for your talent. Best of all, you'll do it in a professional manner – focus on what's really important to both you and the employer. You'll begin building a relationship which should be mutually rewarding as you start a job you really do well and enjoy doing, and one in which the employer gets great value for his or her money. And in the end, that's what this is all about – replaying your predictable pattern of accomplishments for a new employer in exchange for proper compensation.

2

Common Mistakes
You Must Avoid

S AVVY SALARY NEGOTIATORS avoid common job search errors as well as exhibit certain behaviors that lead to salary success. Both unfamiliar and uncomfortable talking about money, many job seekers make errors that result in quickly accepting a compensation package that doesn't reflect their true worth. On the other hand, savvy salary negotiators focus on what's really important to getting a job that is right for them. Above all, they know how to communicate their value to employers and ensure their value is translated into an attractive compensation package. They exhibit a set of positive behaviors that might be best termed "the savvy salary negotiator."

Are You a Savvy Salary Negotiator?

Just how savvy a salary negotiator are you? How prepared are you to negotiate a salary that truly reflects your worth? What knowledge and skills do you need to become a savvy salary negotiator?

Let's start by evaluating your knowledge and skill level for becoming an effective salary negotiator. Respond to the following statements by circling "Yes" or "No." If you are uncertain about your answer, just leave the statement alone and move on to the next statement.

1. I know what I'm worth in comparison to others in today's job market.   Yes   No

2. I know what others make in my company.   Yes   No

3. I can negotiate a salary 15 percent higher than my current salary.   Yes   No

4. I can negotiate a salary 5-10 percent higher than what the employer is prepared to offer me.   Yes   No

5. I know where I can quickly find salary information for my particular position.   Yes   No

6. I usually feel comfortable talking about compensation issues with others, including my boss.   Yes   No

7. I'm familiar with how various compensation options work with most employers, such as signing bonuses, performance bonuses, cafeteria plans, reimbursement accounts, disability insurance, 401(k) Plans, SEPs, CODAs, stock options, flex-time, tuition reimbursement, and severance pay.   Yes   No

8. I understand the different types of stock options and equity incentives offered by employers in my field.   Yes   No

9. I know what my current compensation package is worth when translated into dollar equivalents.   Yes   No

10. I'm prepared to negotiate more than seven different compensation options.   Yes   No

11. I have a list of at least 50 accomplishments and a clear pattern of performance which I can communicate to prospective employers.   Yes   No

12. I'm prepared to tell at least five different
    one- to three-minute stories about my
    proudest achievements.   Yes   No

13. If asked to state my "salary requirements"
    in a cover letter or on an application, I
    know what to write.   Yes   No

14. I know when I should and should not
    discuss salary during an interview.   Yes   No

15. I know what to best say if the interviewer
    asks me _"What are your salary expectations?"_   Yes   No

16. I know what questions to ask during the
    interview in order to get information about
    salaries in the interviewer's company.   Yes   No

17. I know when it's time to stop talking
    and start serious negotiations.   Yes   No

18. I know how to use the "salary range" to
    create "common ground" and strengthen
    my negotiation position.   Yes   No

19. I know how to use silence to strengthen
    my negotiation position.   Yes   No

20. If offered a position, I know what to
    say and do next.   Yes   No

TOTALS   ___   ___

If you responded "No" to more than three of the above statements or "Yes" to fewer than 15 of the statements, you should find this book very useful as you prepare for effectively negotiating a compensation package. Like many job seekers who have followed our principles of salary success, the tips presented here should help you substantially increase your salaried income in the future. Indeed, you may be surprised how effective you are when it comes time to talk money to power!

21 Salary Errors to Avoid

Job seekers typically make several salary negotiation errors, which often result in knocking them out of consideration for the job or receiving and accepting a lower salary offer than what they could have received had they practiced a few of the salary tips outlined in this book. Several of these errors also may leave a bad impression with an employer – that you have a bad attitude, or you are basically a self-centered job seeker who primarily focuses on salary and benefits rather than on the performance needs of the employer and organization. The most frequent errors you should avoid include:

1. **Engaging in wishful thinking – believing you are worth a lot more than you are currently being paid but having no credible evidence of what you really should be paid.**

   Few people will admit they are paid too much. Rather, they often feel they are being paid too little. They even suspect that many of their less talented co-workers may be making more for doing less work. Unless you know for certain that you are being underpaid – conducted research on salary comparables and know exactly what you should be paid for your level of skills and accomplishments – this type of thinking will become a form of self-defeating behavior as you become increasingly unhappy with your job. If you've done your research and know what you are really worth in today's job market, you are well advised to first talk with your boss about adjusting your compensation package rather than start looking for another job that may pay more, even though you still don't know what you're worth.

2. **Approaching the job search as an exercise in being clever and manipulative rather than being clear, correct, and competent in communicating your value to others.**

   Perhaps it's the lack of salary negotiation experience, a fear of failure, or a lack of data that leads some job seekers to engage in extreme gamesmanship. Whatever you do, make sure you approach your prospective employer in as professional a manner as possible. This is not the time to play games or demonstrate how clever you can be in negotiating compensation. Most savvy employers know when they are being manipulated by a clever job seeker. Playing games conveys all the wrong messages about your future behavior with the employer – that you are probably disingenuous, manipulative, and dishonest. Regardless of how good you may be in doing a job, no one wants to hire such individuals. Remember, how well you handle the interview and negotiate your salary sets the tone for developing important on-the-job relationships.

> *Playing games gives the wrong messages about your future behavior with the employer.*

3. **Failing to research salary options and comparables and thus having few supports to justify your worth.**

You best negotiate from strength when you have salary data that **supports** your negotiating position. You can easily get such data on the Internet, through your local library, or by talking with individuals who are willing to share such information. Indeed, it only takes a few minutes on the Internet to find useful salary information by visiting such sites as www.salary.com, www.job smart.org, www.wageweb.com, and www.salarysource.com. Our advice: never talk about salary with a potential employer before doing basic salary research on the value of the position for which you are interviewing.

4. **Fail to compile a list of specific accomplishments, including anecdotal one- to three-minute performance stories, that provide evidence of your value to employers.**

Another way of providing supports for your negotiating position is to talk about your specific accomplishments with interesting stories and examples. If you are in sales, for example, can you talk about how you improved sales by 50 percent in six months? Can you tell a story about how you turned around a client who left your company? Can you tell five stories about the most satisfying moments in your career? Can you explain what really turns you on? If not, it's time to begin putting together a portfolio of accomplishments and related stories.

5. Revealing salary expectations on the resume or in a letter.

You should never reveal your expectations prior to interviewing for a job unless you want to quickly eliminate certain employers from consideration. However, this works both ways. On the process of revealing your salary expectations, you set certain limitations on your future negotiating position and may actually be knocked out of consideration. For example, if you state on your resume or in a letter that you expect a salary of $60,000 but the employer has the position budgeted at $80,000, one of two things might happen. First, you may not be considered for the position because you appear unqualified for it because of your expected pay level. Second, the employer may feel he or she can get a real bargain by offering you only $60,000 for a position that was thought to cost $80,000. Either way, you put yourself at a disadvantage by stating your salary expectations.

6. Prematurely talking about salary by answering the question *"What are your salary requirements?"* before being offered the job.

Employers often raise the salary question early in the interview. They may actually do this during a telephone screening interview. Their basic goal is to either screen you into or out of consideration for the position on salary criteria. Like stating your salary expectations on a resume or in a cover letter, responding to this question with a figure early in the interview puts you at a disadvantage. The old poker saying that *"He who reveals his hand first is at a disadvantage"* is especially true when negotiating salary. Time should work in your favor. After all, you need more information about the job and your responsibilities in order to determine the value of the position. Is the job really worth $60,000, $80,000, $100,000, or more? A job worth $100,000 a year has different levels of responsibility than one worth only $60,000 a year. If the employer raises the salary expectation questions early in the interview, it's best to respond by saying *"I really need to know more about the position and my responsibilities before I can discuss compensation. Can you tell me about . . . ?"* This response will usually result in postponing the salary question and impress upon the employer that you are a thoughtful professional who is more employer-centered than self-centered with your interest in the position. Salary should be the very last thing you talk about – within the context of a job offer, which may be after two or three inter-

> *Salary should be the very last thing you talk about – within the context of a job offer, which may be after two or three interviews.*

views. Once you have been offered the job, then talk about compensation. In other words, no offer, no salary discussion.

7. **Raising the salary question rather than waiting for the employer to do so.**

If you really want to appear self-centered and impress upon the employer that you are primarily interested in the money, go ahead and ask about the salary being offered. When you prematurely raise the salary question, you begin re-focusing the job interview on your needs, and possible greed. And there's nothing worse for an employer than to hire a self-centered individual who appears needy and greedy in the job interview. By asking this question, you raise a red flag that can knock you out of further consideration – you may not be called back for another interview. The irony of salary negotiations is that you are most likely to be offered a higher salary if you don't talk about salary, until forced to do so at the very end of the interview process which could be 10, 20, or 30 days after your initial interview. And when you do finally talk about salary, you should listen and pause a great deal rather than talk a lot about compensation. Your near silence may be handsomely rewarded! Again, he who reveals his hand first will most likely be at a financial disadvantage in the end.

8. Failing to ask questions about the company, job, and previous occupants of the position.

Self-centered candidates who primarily focus on salary and benefits, and frequently appear needy and greedy during the job interview, often fail to focus on the basics of employment. Many of them prepare for the job interview by developing canned answers to anticipated interview questions. Worst of all, they fail to ask questions which indicate an interest in the organization, employer, and job. By asking questions you also learn how to value the position – you discover what it's really worth compared to similar positions in other organizations. If, for example, a $75,000 position involves supervising 10 people with budgetary responsibilities of $1 million but you discover during the interview that you would be expected to supervise 50 people with budgetary responsibilities of $10 million, perhaps the value of the position should be much higher. But you won't be able to value this position unless you've done research on salary comparables as well as asked questions, including what exactly the past occupant of this position was expected to do and did or did not do according to expectations. For example, you might ask *"Can you tell me a little bit about the last person who held this position. What exactly did she do? What changes do you envision?"* These questions can later be expanded into a salary-related question: *"From what I've heard about this position, what would someone with my qualifications expect to earn here?"* This question turns the tables and asks the employer to volunteer a salary figure or range.

9. Asking *"Is this offer negotiable?"*

Unless you are interviewing for an entry-level or government position, where salaries are relatively set, you should assume most salaries are somewhat negotiable. Most employers have some flexibility to negotiate both salary and benefits, although they may have more flexibility on the benefit side of the compensation equation. In addition, you may want to negotiate other aspects of the job which may normally not be part of a standard job offer, such as a signing bonus, incentivized pay scheme, cell phone, laptop computer, and flexible hours. By asking this question – whether the offer is negotiable rather than assuming that aspects of it will be – you tend to immediately lose the advantage in the negotiation process.

10. **Quickly accepting the first offer, believing that's what the position is really worth and that an employer might be offended if one tries to negotiate.**

First offers are exactly that – initial offers. Employers may be prepared to extend second, third, fourth, and fifth offers, depending on your negotiating skills. Since most salaries are negotiable, you tend to diminish your value by not taking your time to think over a first offer and then negotiating the final terms of employment. In fact, since many employers expect candidates to negotiate, their first offer is usually their lowest offer. Employers also tend to respect candidates who come prepared to the salary negotiation session, present evidence of their value, and negotiate in a professional manner. In the process, they learn a great deal about their new employee.

> *Since many employers expect candidates to negotiate, their first offer is usually their lowest offer.*

11. **Accepting the offer on the spot.**

Timing is everything when negotiating salary. Timing can take several forms, from pausing to consider the offer to asking for 24 to 48 hours to think over the offer. Many of our associates report excellent results by pausing in silence for 30 seconds after receiving an initial offer – the pregnant pause that often makes the employer feel uneasy about what he senses may be seen as a low offer. This pause can result in an increase in several thousands of dollars in a second offer which can immediately come at the end of the 30-second pause. At the same time, it's common professional courtesy to ask for at least 24 hours to consider the offer. During that time, you can do additional research on salary comparables, check with other employers with whom you may have interviewed and, if you choose to, develop a well organized counter-offer.

12. Accepting the offer primarily because of compensation.

If you only focus on salary and benefits, you may be disappointed and unhappy with the job. Research continues to show that salary and benefits rank fourth and fifth in the order of importance when valuing jobs. The nature of the work, the culture of the organization, and people you work with are often more important than salary and benefits. You should focus on learning as much as possible about the nature of the job and organization as well as the people you would be working with. You do this by asking lots of questions about the company and the job. Answers to their questions should indicate whether this job is a perfect fit for you. Is this something you can do well and enjoy doing? Will it allow you to pursue your passion? If the answers are "yes," chances are you'll be able to negotiate a satisfactory compensation package. After all, the employer also should know, based upon your previous accomplishments and interests, that you will be a good fit for the company. Your productivity will more than justify the compensation.

13. Trying to negotiate compensation during the first interview.

Today, many candidates go through three to seven interviews with an employer before receiving a job offer. The first interview seldom deals with the money question, although this question can arise at anytime to screen someone into or out of consideration. Again, you should never raise the salary issue, for to do so puts you at a disadvantage. Expect the salary offer, and accompanying salary negotiations, to take place during the final interview. The sign of when you should talk seriously about money is when you are offered the job. The offer comes first followed by discussion of appropriate compensation. Another way of handling the *"What are your salary requirements?"* question is to respond by asking *"Are you offering me the position?"* If the response is *"No,"* then you might respond by saying *"I really need to know more about the position and your company before I feel comfortable discussing compensation."* Alternatively, you might want to use this occasion to do research on the company's salary structure by asking *"By the way, how much are you paying at present for this position?"* Always try to get the employer to volunteer salary information from which you can formulate your response.

14. Forgetting to calculate the value of benefits and thus only focusing on the gross salary figure.

Benefits can account for 40 percent or more of a total compensation package, depending on the company. Therefore, you are well advised to calculate your current compensation package and separate your gross salary figure from the benefits. For example, is your current compensation package worth $90,000, with a $60,000 base salary? If so, you should figure at least $30,000 in benefits or one-third of your total compensation package as being in benefits. You may discover your next employer is prepared to offer you a $70,000 base salary with $20,000 in benefits, which means the new position is equivalent to your present position.

15. Focusing on benefits, stock options, and perks rather than on the gross salary figure.

This is the logical corollary to Error #14. While benefits, stock options, and perks can add up to a significant percentage of one's total compensation, at the same time, many of these "extras" come with the job regardless of your negotiation skills. In other words, everyone at your pay level may receive the same benefits, stock options, and perks. Therefore, you need to determine what exactly comes with the job versus those things that are negotiable. Base salary is usually negotiable and thus it should be your main focus for negotiation. Don't be overly impressed with the "extras" if they merely come with the job. Start by getting an overall understanding of what components make up the company's compensation package and how each of the components translates into cash. Start negotiating the base salary and then move on to other elements in the compensation package. As many dot-comers of 2000-2001 can testify, don't be overly impressed with stock options since they may be worthless, if not costly, by the time you get ready to exercise them or during the time you hold them.

16. Trying to negotiate a specific salary figure rather than talking about a salary range.

Savvy salary negotiators always talk about "salary ranges" rather than specific salary figures. They do so because ranges give them flexibility in the negotiation process. If, for example, you get the employer to reveal his or her hand first by saying the job pays $75,000 a year, if you are interested, you should counter by putting the employer's figure at the bottom of your range – *"Based on my salary research as well as my experience, I was thinking more in terms of $75,000 to $85,000 a year."* By doing this, you establish common ground from which to negotiate the figure upwards toward the high end of your range. While the employer may not want to pay more than $75,000, he or she at least knows you are within budget. The employer most likely will counter by saying, *"Well, we might be able to go $78,000."* You, in turn, can counter by saying *"Is it possible to go $81,000?"* As you will quickly discover in the salary negotiation business, anything is "possible" if you handle the situation professionally – with supports and flexibility. In this situation, you might have been able to negotiate a $6,000 increase over the employer's initial offer because you established common ground with a salary range and then moved the employer toward the upper end of your range because you had supports and professional appeal.

17. Negotiating over the telephone or by e-mail.

Compensation is a serious business that requires face-to-face meetings to work out the details. When you negotiate, you are on stage presenting your best professional self. You're giving a presentation about yourself and the job as well as providing supports, which may be in paper form, to justify your salary expectations. Only use the telephone and e-mail if you're really not serious about the position and thus don't want to waste your time in another meeting.

18. Talking too much and listening too little.

Employers report one of the major failings of job candidates is talking too much. For some candidates, much of this problem is related to nervousness – they talk and talk and talk as if they are giving evidence that they are honest, social, interested, and receptive to the employer. From the interviewer's perspective, such excessive talkers are likely to be self-centered, irritating,

> *Excessive talkers are likely to be self-centered, irritating, and failures at listening.*

and failures at listening. If they talk this much in the interview, what will they do once they are on the job? Excessive talkers also tend to say the wrong things about salary and benefits. They have a tendency to talk about their needs rather than the needs of the employer.

19. Focusing on your needs rather than the employer's needs.

There's nothing worse you can do than to focus on your financial needs when negotiating salary, such as you need to make X number of dollars because you're buying a new house or car, your spouse is pregnant, your parents need medical attention, or you're sending two children to college next year, which is a real financial burden. That's your problem – not the employer's. After all, the employer is not hiring you as a social experiment! Indeed, by focusing on your financial needs, you may be communicating a terrible message – that you are financially irresponsible and way over your head financially. Not only is that a very self-centered approach, it also communicates that you are probably needy and greedy. Given your personal financial situation, you'll probably "need" a raise in no time! You should always focus your attention on the needs of the employer and what you plan to do for him or her in terms of **outcomes**. Always justify a higher salary figure in terms of your salary research and your predictable pattern of performance. If, for example, you expect to earn $100,000 a year, but the employer only offers $80,000 a year, present a plan in which you show that your work over the next year will generate $400,000 rather than $300,000 in additional income or that you will be saving the employer X number of dollars that more than justify your expected salary. Remember, most employers want one or two major outcomes from people they hire: (1) generate more income, or (2) save money for the company. In other words, your presence should significantly make or save money for the employer.

20. Trying to play "hardball."

Playing hardball and being demanding in salary negotiations can backfire. Doing so also can be very revealing of one's motivations and capabilities. Some candidates prefer to lie about their past salary history, exaggerate their accomplishments, or claim they have alternative job offers waiting in the wings. Treating employers as a combination of adversaries and fools, such job seekers play a very chancy game of "hard to get." If this is the route you choose to go in order to "win" the salary game – rather than being honest, forthright, and professional in your dealings with an employer – chances are you will play similar unethical games once you're on the job. And chances are you are headed for trouble on your new job since you probably have a pattern of developing relationships on such self-centered grounds. In the end, when performance measures your professionalism, no one will really want you because you simply aren't what you say you are. The Emperor really has no clothes. Keep your resume current since you may need to market yourself again soon!

21. Expressing a negative attitude toward the employer's offer.

Throughout the interview, and especially during the salary negotiation session, your attitude is on display. How you respond to the employer's offer is an important indicator of how you will most likely deal with the employer in the future. Never show your displeasure, shock, or anger at a lower than expected offer. Always try to convey the impression that you are a professional – you've done your homework, present your case with supports, and explain what it will take to attract you. You also may need to be tough – hold the line on what you want and be prepared to walk away from the negotiation table if the employer does not value you the way you value yourself and the position.

Seven Behaviors of Savvy Negotiators

Savvy salary negotiators tend to display seven key behaviors that contribute to success. These behaviors can be learned by following the many techniques outlined in the remainder of this book. The following behaviors are associated with savvy salary negotiators:

1. **Approach the job search as a process of finding a job that is a perfect "fit" for their motivational pattern – one they do well and enjoy doing.** While compensation is important, it is not the primary motivator for savvy salary negotiators. Many things may turn them on, but **pursuing a passion** is the primary motivator. They clearly communicate their passion and competence to employers who, in turn, recognize their value and compensate them accordingly.

2. **Conduct research on salary options and salary comparables.** Savvy salary negotiators become very knowledgeable about their market value by conducting salary research. They do so by using the Internet and libraries and by interviewing informed individuals.

3. **Focus on the requirements of the job and the needs of the employer.** Savvy salary negotiators are employer-centered rather than self-centered. They talk the language of employers which focuses on their bottom line – accomplishments, benefits, and performance.

4. **Ask lots of questions about the company, employer, and position as well as listen carefully.** Savvy salary negotiators view the interview as an exchange of information between the candidate and the employer. They understand that both parties need to determine whether or not this will be a good "fit." Asking questions and listening carefully to the interviewer are the major communication techniques they use for acquiring critical information about the company, employer, and position.

5. **Emphasize their value throughout the interview.** Savvy salary negotiators focus on their accomplishments throughout each and every interview. They emphasize through examples, statistics, and short anecdotes that they have a clear pattern of accomplishments related to their motivational pattern or passion. They also send thank you letters which emphasize their social graces and likability.

6. **Use timing and silence to their advantage.** Savvy salary negotiators talk seriously about money only after receiving an offer. Knowing the importance of acquiring information about the job and stressing their value throughout the interview, they avoid prematurely discussing compensation. When offered the job and negotiating the salary figure, they know silence is golden by using the "30-second pause" to their advantage.

7. **Focus on the total compensation package rather than just the gross salary figure.** Savvy salary negotiators know there is much more to compensation than just a salary figure. They learn to talk intelligently about compensation options, including a variety of benefits, stock options, and equity incentives. They are prepared to offer creative win-win compensation options.

Taken together, these behaviors should result in negotiating a compensation package that truly reflects your value as well as cements a positive relationship with your new employer. When the employer says *"You're hired,"* you'll say *"This is the perfect job – great place, great job, great people, great compensation."* It doesn't get much better than that!

3

Major Compensation Options and Issues

I N TODAY'S JOB MARKET, compensation takes on many different forms in addition to base salary. In general, the larger the organization and higher the level of the position, the more compensation options available. For example, a company with 1,000 or more employees is more likely to offer on-site and/or backup child care services than a company with only 50 employees. At the same time, negotiation flexibility tends to be greater with higher level positions – those paying in excess of $50,000 a year.

Know What You're Worth

Calculating what you're really worth in today's job market requires understanding the full compensation picture, which includes base salary, bonuses, stock options, benefits, perks, and other forms of compensation. You first need to calculate what your past and present jobs were worth in order to provide an honest answer to one of the most commonly asked questions of job candidates – *"What's your salary history?"* You may be surprised to discover that your last job which paid a base salary of $40,000 was actually worth $70,000 when you included bonuses, stock options, dental insurance, 401(k) plan, tuition reimbursement, cellular phone, a laptop computer, DSL and wireless Internet service, and discount travel. You need to go through the same calculation when considering the value of a job for which you have received an offer.

Decide What's Important to You

Once you calculate the value of a position by examining various compensation options, you need to decide what is more or less important to you and your future. Are you primarily interested in cash or do you also place a great deal of value on dental insurance, profit sharing, and time off? For example, if you are single and well educated, you may have no interest in child care services or tuition reimbursement. But you may be especially interested in the base salary, bonuses, stock options, athletic club membership, and disability insurance. On the other hand, if you are a single parent with young children, you may be especially interested in on-site child care, personal and family leave, flextime, medical and dental insurance, and company discounts. If you are in a high income bracket, you may want to explore cash or deferred arrangements (CODAs) and a 401(k) plan. Your personal situation will determine what's important to you.

> *Today more and more employers are experimenting with flexible compensation packages.*

Today more and more employers are experimenting with flexible compensation packages. Many employers now offer cafeteria plans which enable employees to pick and choose a mix of benefits that best meet their needs. Some employees, for example, may need on-site child care services but not medical and dental insurance since they are already covered on their spouse's policy. Other employees may find tuition reimbursement to be a very attractive benefit for furthering their education and training but they have no need for flex time, parking privileges, or a health club membership. All of these benefits and perks add up to real money when translated into dollar equivalents. They may or may not be important to you, but they all cost money, which should be reflected in your compensation package.

Examine What's Being Offered

Hopefully, the employer will offer numerous compensation options from which you can pick and choose what best meets your needs. Once you enter into negotiations, one of the first questions you need to ask concerns all the elements in the compensation package. What exactly is the employer offering in addition to a base salary? How much are these elements worth if translated into cash? Which elements are negotiable and how much flexibility does the employer have in negotiating individual elements. If, for example, you already have medical and dental coverage under your spouse's employer, can you exchange this benefit for a higher base salary, more stock options, or increased personal leave days? After all, by not taking medical and dental insurance, you may save the employer $5,000 to $10,000 a year in insurance costs and thus decrease your overall compensation by that much if you do not take this or some equivalent benefit.

Negotiate Base Pay

When all is said and done, base pay still remains the major indicator of your value and the value of positions, as well as the basis for comparing the value of different positions. Base pay is your "salary" – take-home pay plus all the deductions that show up in the pay stub of your regular paycheck. You can usually expect base pay to represent 60 to 80 percent of a total compensation package. While you may focus most of your attention on negotiating base pay, don't forget that there's another 20 to 40 percent in a compensation package that may also be negotiable. Depending on how you structure your compensation package, especially with bonuses, incentivized pay schemes, and stock options, this part of a compensation package can well exceed the 20 to 40 percent range. Indeed, many executives manage to structure compensation packages in which base pay may only represent 20 percent of their total compensation! We've all heard of the major CEO who earns $750,000 a year in base pay but walks away with more than $10 million in annual compensation because of generous bonuses and exercised stock options.

Consider Bonuses

Bonuses can come in many forms, from an initial signing bonus to a quarterly or annual performance bonus. Depending on market conditions and the level of a position, many employers offer **signing bonuses** which are used to lure you away from a current employer, assist with relocation expenses, or offer a financial incentive over the competition. Signing bonuses can range from a nominal $1,000 for an entry-level position to $20,000 or higher for a more senior position. Many signing bonuses run in the $3,000 to $5,000 range, representing the equivalent of one month's salary.

Make sure the bonus discussion focuses on your performance rather than the overall performance of the organization or that of a team.

When in doubt whether or not an employer offers a signing bonus, just ask this question during the negotiation session: *"Would I expect to be offered a signing bonus?"* But raising this question prior to receiving a job offer communicates the wrong message – you have bills to pay, or you are primarily interested in instant monetary gratification! Instead, reserve this question for the negotiation session, which occurs after receiving a job offer.

Be sure to ask about **performance bonuses related to your productivity**. After all, you are presenting yourself as someone who produces results. You should receive a bonus for achieving results that are above your expected pay grade. Make sure the bonus discussion focuses on your performance rather than the overall performance of the organization or that of a team, since you have little control over the performance of others. Despite all the trendy talk about team efforts and being a team player, you should still focus on receiving extra rewards in the form of a bonus for your individual performance when it exceeds the employer's expectations. For individuals making in excess of $75,000 a year, bonuses can range from $3,000 to $30,000 or more a year, depending on how both you and the company structure bonuses.

Calculate Benefits

Benefits can come in many different forms, depending on the organization. The most widely offered benefits include the following:

- Insurance:
  - medical
  - dental
  - vision
  - life
  - disability
- Reimbursement accounts
- Financial/retirement plans:
  - 401(k) plan
  - Simplified Employee Pension (SEP)
  - Cash or deferred arrangement (CODA)
  - Pension or annuity
  - Profit sharing
  - Stock options
- Days off:
  - Vacation
  - Sick leave
  - Personal leave
  - Holidays
- Child care:
  - On-site
  - Backup

The big ticket item for employers is insurance, a benefit whose costs have dramatically increased within the past decade. Many employers offer 100 percent coverage on medical and dental insurance while others may offer partial coverage, such as 80 percent. Depending on how important these benefits are to you, they can add up to a substantial amount of compensation.

Be sure to examine your financial investment and retirement options, especially stock options, profit sharing, 401(k) plans, deferred compensation plans, and equity participation.

Understand Stock Options

Stock options have recently become a hot salary negotiation topic, especially in the dot-com world before it crashed in 2001. Indeed, many people who settled for low base salaries in exchange for wishful windfall stock options discovered they actually negotiated "sloptions" rather than promising stock options – a term accurately reflecting the reality of stock options that became worthless when it came time to exercise them.

Nonetheless, stock options still remain an important subject for negotiating compensation packages. However, not all stock options are equal. Some have serious tax consequences which you should know about before settling for what may turn out to be a very negative tax burden should the stock significantly decline. While stock options used to be reserved for senior executives, today various stock option plans may be offered to all employees in an organization. A company may provide all of these stock option plans simultaneously to their employees at all levels: incentive stock options, nonqualified stock options, stock grants, stock appreciation rights, phantom stock options, and stock purchase plans. Be sure you understand the tax implications of the various plans as well as the vested period. For example, some liberal companies allow employees to exercise 20 percent of their stock options at the end of their first year of employment and then another 40 percent during each of the next two years. Other companies may require a three-year employment or "vesting" period before exercising stock options.

> *Be sure you understand the tax implications of the various stock option plans as well as the vesting period.*

Equity Incentives

Executive-level candidates are often offered equity participation in a company in exchange for a lower salary – a percentage ownership of the company. Like stock options, this is a risky compensation element which can prove to be a financial bonanza should the company become very successful and you are able to sell your equity to the highest bidder. On the other hand, if the company does not do well, this could be a costly benefit since you probably accepted a lower salary in exchange for such equity participation. Equity in a company is not a liquid asset.

Profit Sharing

Many employers offer profit sharing plans. Usually 100 percent funded by the employer, these plans set aside a certain percentage of the company's annual profits into individual profit sharing accounts. Operating similarly to 401(k) plans, many profit sharing plans are deferred contribution plans – not taxable until the employee decides to take cash out of the account. But not all profit sharing plans are the same, nor do they benefit everyone. Depending on the company, they may operate as tax shelters for deferring hidden compensation of top executives. One of your concerns should be to understand how the company's profit sharing plan has operated in the past, especially who benefits and by how much. In some companies, the profit sharing plan may be deliberately structured to distribute 80 percent of the profits to the top five percent of the employees. If you're not in the top five percent, your profit sharing benefits may be insignificant. For example, what has been the company's track record during the past five years? Has it fully funded the profit sharing plan? Assuming one made $70,000 a year, how much would one's profit sharing account be worth over the past five years? Answers to these questions will tell you a lot about the profitability of the company as well as how well the plan is structured to benefit employees at your salary level. You'll also get some idea as to the dollar value of the profit sharing plan and an understanding of how it has operated in recent years.

401(k) Plans

Within the past decade more and more employers have offered 401(k) plans to their employees. Operating similarly to IRAs in terms of tax deferred income, this is a particularly attractive benefit when the employer contributes a percentage to the plan and especially when the stock market is booming. Indeed, during the late 1990s, many employees were pleasantly surprised to discover their 401(k) plans were increasing at an annual rate of 10 to 30 percent. During an economic downturn, these plans are less attractive. Indeed, they look like risky business for employees who prefer immediate cash to deferred income.

Deferred Compensation Plans

Deferred compensation plans are often used for top executives who prefer deferring a portion of their income into their retirement years when their tax liabilities may be less than during their high income years. These plans require a contractual agreement between the employer and employee in order to meet IRS requirements. Many employers are receptive to these plans since they promote long-term commitment and loyalty to the company.

Perks

Employment perks can be powerful motivators to join, as well as remain with, a company. The particular mix of perks can vary dramatically from one company to another and add up to a substantial financial advantage. How important these perks are to you depends on your personal and professional situation. For example, do you need a laptop computer, DSL connection, and cell phone – perks that may be valued at over $5,000 in additional annual compensation? What about free parking, club memberships, professional dues, company discounts, tuition reimbursement, free tickets to events, and incentive trips? Employers offer many of the following perks which translate into real money for employees:

- Moving expenses
- Free parking
- Car allowance
- Laptop computer
- Cell phone
- Hand-held communication devices
- DSL line and wireless Internet connection
- Flex-time and extra leave

- Tuition reimbursement for you and family
- Free drinks and meals
- Upgraded business travel
- Frequent flyer miles
- Travel reimbursement
- Paid travel for spouse
- Free or discounted memberships or services
- Company health club
- Discounts on company products
- Moving expenses
- Sabbaticals
- Incentive trips
- Office with a window

Severance Package

Like any relationship, jobs don't last forever. They eventually break up or die. Given today's volatile job market and turbulent economy, you never know what might happen to that great job you've just been offered. While you may paint wonderful scenarios of this terrific company, your impending success, and all the warm and talented people you will be working with, the reality is that this is business and business has its human and monetary cycles. Your "parting company" may come when the company downsizes or your current or future boss decides you no longer "fit" into the organization, be it for personal, political, or performance reasons. You may be given 30 minutes to clean out your desk and pick up your final paycheck or two to four weeks to leave the company. Being laid off or fired are part of life in the employment arena. When it happens, you should have an agreement in place as to how you will depart the organization. Many companies include in their employment agreements provisions for parting company. Top level executives may have "golden parachutes" which can translate into hundreds of thousands, if not millions, of dollars. Such parachutes include provisions for 6-12 months of base pay, prorated bonuses and incentives, cashing in stock and equity, voice mail access, vacation reimbursement, outplacement assistance, and the continuation of health benefits and 401(k) contributions. Lower-level employees may have a severance agreement which provides two, four, or eight weeks of pay for making the job transition. The agreement might also include a provision for job counseling and outplacement services or a continuation of medical, dental, and life insurance.

Checklist of Compensation Options

When it's time to talk about compensation with an employer, it's always a good idea to prepare a written statement of your current, or previous, compensation package. This statement should summarize the various elements included in your compensation package as well as the value of each. Some elements, such as an office with a window, may not have a dollar value but they are important to you.

One of the easiest ways to survey your compensation options and assign value to your ideal compensation package is to use the following checklist of compensation options. Consider each item and then value it by assigning a dollar amount. When finished, add up the total dollars assigned to get a complete picture of the value of your present or past compensation package.

Element	Value

Basic Compensation Issues

❑ Base salary $ _____
❑ Commissions $ _____
❑ Corporate profit sharing $ _____
❑ Personal performance bonuses/incentives $ _____
❑ Cost of living adjustment $ _____
❑ Overtime $ _____
❑ Signing bonus $ _____
❑ Cash in lieu of certain benefits $ _____

Health Benefits

❑ Medical insurance $ _____
❑ Dental insurance $ _____
❑ Vision insurance $ _____

❏ Prescription package $ _____
❏ Life insurance $ _____
❏ Accidental death and disability insurance $ _____
❏ Evacuation insurance (international travel) $ _____

Vacation and Time Issues

❏ Vacation time $ _____
❏ Sick days $ _____
❏ Personal time $ _____
❏ Holidays $ _____
❏ Flex-time $ _____
❏ Compensatory time $ _____
❏ Paternity/maternity leave $ _____
❏ Family leave $ _____

Retirement-Oriented Benefits

❏ Defined benefit plan $ _____
❏ 401(k) plan $ _____
❏ Deferred compensation $ _____
❏ Savings plans $ _____
❏ Stock-purchase plans $ _____
❏ Stock bonus $ _____
❏ Stock options $ _____
❏ Ownership/equity $ _____

Education

❏ Professional continuing education $ _____
❏ Tuition reimbursement for you or your
   family members $ _____

Military

❏ Compensatory pay during active duty $ _____
❏ National Guard $ _____

Perquisites

❑ Cellular phone $ _____
❑ Company car or vehicle/mileage allowance $ _____
❑ Expense accounts $ _____
❑ Liberalization of business-related expenses $ _____
❑ Child care $ _____
❑ Cafeteria privileges $ _____
❑ Executive dining room privileges $ _____
❑ First-class hotels $ _____
❑ First-class air travel $ _____
❑ Upgrade business travel $ _____
❑ Personal use of frequent-flyer awards $ _____
❑ Convention participation: professionally related $ _____
❑ Parking $ _____
❑ Paid travel for spouse $ _____
❑ Professional association memberships $ _____
❑ Athletic club memberships $ _____
❑ Social club memberships $ _____
❑ Use of company-owned facilities $ _____
❑ Executive office $ _____
❑ Office with a window $ _____
❑ Laptop computers $ _____
❑ Private secretary $ _____
❑ Portable fax $ _____
❑ Employee discounts $ _____
❑ Incentive trips $ _____
❑ Sabbaticals $ _____
❑ Discounted buying club memberships $ _____
❑ Free drinks and meals $ _____

Relocation Expenses

❑ Direct moving expenses $ _____
❑ Moving costs for unusual property $ _____
❑ Trips to find suitable housing $ _____
❑ Loss on sale of present home
   or lease termination $ _____

❑ Company handling sale of present home $ _____
❑ Housing cost differential between cities $ _____
❑ Mortgage rate differential $ _____
❑ Mortgage fees and closing costs $ _____
❑ Temporary dual housing $ _____
❑ Trips home during dual residency $ _____
❑ Real estate fees $ _____
❑ Utilities hookup $ _____
❑ Drapes/carpets $ _____
❑ Appliance installation $ _____
❑ Auto/pet shipping $ _____
❑ Signing bonus for incidental expenses $ _____
❑ Additional meals expense account $ _____
❑ Bridge loan while owning two homes $ _____
❑ Outplacement assistance for spouse $ _____

Home Office Options

❑ Personal computer $ _____
❑ Internet access $ _____
❑ Copier $ _____
❑ Printer $ _____
❑ Financial planning assistance $ _____
❑ Separate phone line $ _____
❑ Separate fax line $ _____
❑ CPA/tax assistance $ _____
❑ Incidental/support office functions $ _____
❑ Office supplies $ _____
❑ Furniture and accessories $ _____

Severance Packages (Parachutes)

❑ Base salary $ _____
❑ Bonuses/incentives $ _____
❑ Non-compete clause $ _____
❑ Stock/equity $ _____
❑ Outplacement assistance $ _____
❑ Voice mail access $ _____

❑ Statement (letter) explaining why you left $ _____
❑ Vacation reimbursement $ _____
❑ Health benefits or reimbursements $ _____
❑ 401(k) contributions $ _____

TOTAL $

Once you've completed this exercise, you should be well prepared to negotiate various aspects of your compensation package. You'll know exactly what you have been worth in the past as well as have a good idea of how to calculate the total value of the position in question.

4

Calculate Your Worth

Wmarket? Is it more or less than you are getting at
present or in your most recent job? If you can't answer
these questions with a specific dollar figure, as well as
discuss benefits and perks appropriate for someone with your qualifications, you will be at a disadvantage when it comes time to negotiate your compensation package. You may be valued by employers at
much less than what you should be worth.

Consider the Employer's Perspective

By the very fact they are hiring, employers have a problem to solve –
find the right talent for a specific position that contributes to the
company's performance. You can assume most employers are both
rational and reasonable about money, although some may lack comparative salary information from which to make a rational decision!
Unfamiliar with what other employers are paying for comparable
positions, they may initially offer a lower than expected salary figure.
While they would prefer hiring someone who does not cost a great
deal, they know top talent for solving their problems costs money,
perhaps more than they are prepared to pay. Many do not want to pay

a new hire more than a 15 percent increase over his or her last salary, a figure that represents talent at the appropriate pay level. At the same time, they do not want to develop a reputation for being a cheap or exploitive employer, nor do they want to be the salary leader for your type of position. They prefer paying the "norm," which is the going market rate based upon an understanding of what other employers pay for such positions. They may ask early on in the interview about your salary history or salary requirements in order to screen you into or out of consideration. They want to know if you are at the appropriate pay level and if they can afford you.

> *Employers may ask early on in the interview about your salary history or salary requirements in order to screen you into or out of further consideration.*

Knowing the employer's perspective – rational but perhaps uninformed about salary comparables – you can expect most employers have room to negotiate salaries. After all, they need to solve a problem which they know will cost money. If they decide you are their top candidate – the person who has exceptional talent to solve their problem – they will make a good effort to attract you to their company by negotiating an attractive compensation package. As long as your negotiating position is considered "reasonable" – it reflects the salary norm for comparable positions in other organizations – you should have room to negotiate a satisfactory compensation package. However, should your salary demands appear unreasonable, because they exceed the norm for comparable positions, expect to encounter difficulties in negotiating a compensation package.

Look At the Big Picture

Once you narrow your choices to a single employer and begin negotiating a compensation package, the tendency is to lose sight of the larger picture of the employer, the company, the position, and your future career. Indeed, you may become preoccupied with negotiating minor issues. As you approach the compensation issue, try to keep the big picture in mind. This picture comes in two forms:

1. The immediate value of the total compensation package.

2. The long-term value of you and the position to the company.

While you should initially focus on negotiating the major cash elements in your compensation package – base salary, bonuses, and commissions – keep in mind the many benefits and perks outlined in Chapter 3 also can have substantial cash value, especially since most are nontaxable. In other words, if your base salary, bonuses, and commissions add up to $75,000 a year, your actual take-home pay may be closer to $50,000 because of federal and state tax obligations. However, you may receive an additional $25,000 in benefits and perks which are nontaxable. If these benefits and perks were given in cash, they would probably be worth $40,000 in before-tax dollars. The point here is to keep the big financial picture in mind when considering your compensation package. You may be worth a lot more than just the taxable dollars you receive from the employer.

At the same time, take a long-term look at the position and the company. What, for example, can you expect to be earning in six months, one year, three years, or five years? You need to get some sense of how your income will grow in the future with this employer. Will you merely receive annual cost-of-living adjustments (COLAs) calculated as a percentage of your base salary, or is there a regular performance or salary review where salary increases are tied to performance? What happened to previous employees in this position? Were they promoted to other positions? Is this a normal career progression in this company? If incumbents got promoted, what were they earning after five years with the company? Again, think about the larger picture with this employer.

Determine Your Market Value

So how do you plan to determine your market value and then communicate it to employers? Your market value to both you and the employer is basically a function of four calculations:

1. **Your recent salary history.** What you've made with previous employers in comparable positions is often a good indicator,

within a 10 to 20 percent range, of your market value. Employers want to know your salary history to see if you are interviewing at the appropriate level for their company. Obviously, someone who interviews for a $75,000 a year job but only makes $35,000 a year in his most recent job probably is not worth a $40,000 salary increase. Most employers will not be happy interviewing someone with such a wide salary discrepancy, regardless of how well they perform in the interview. Such individuals may appear "unqualified" for the job because they are not at the proper pay grade. Employers want to pay you close to what you were making on your last job, with perhaps a 10 to 20 percent increase to persuade you to leave your current position. They are not in the business of giving strangers huge raises!

2. **What the employer is currently paying for the position.** Remember, like employees, positions also have a salary history. You are being hired to fill a position which is more or less budgeted around the same figure given to the current or previous occupant of the position. That figure has probably grown by three to seven percent a year due to annual cost-of-living adjustments as well as increased responsibilities and performance of the previous occupants.

3. **What other employers currently pay for comparable positions.** While employers may have a good idea of what they should pay for a position – based upon the salary history of the position within their organization – they may be less knowledgeable about what other companies, including their competition, are paying for similar positions. Therefore, your job is to research salary comparables and then let the employer know what the "going rate" is in today's job market. You obviously want to be paid at or above the going rate – never below. You can easily conduct this research by:

   ▪ visiting a few key websites, such as www.salary.com, www. jobsmart.org, www.bls.gov, www.salarysource.com, www. wageweb.com, and www.abbott-langer.com.

- contacting your professional association for information on salary ranges. Many associations conduct annual salary surveys.

- networking with individuals who are knowledgeable about salary ranges.

- contacting your local library for salary surveys and studies conducted by various government agencies.

4. **Your perceived future value to the company.** Remember, employers hire new people because they have problems to solve – the last employee didn't work out, it's a new position, or Ms. X was promoted. Assuming they can reach a salary agreement, employers plan to hire you because of your perceived value. Based on an understanding of your past patterns of performance, which you've communicated as a history of key accomplishments, they should be able to project your value over the next 12 months. If, for example, you are being hired for a sales and marketing position, they may expect you to do $1 million in new business over the next 12 months for a base salary of $50,000 plus a five-percent sales commission and performance bonus.

> _Most employers base their salary offer on your salary history and the salary history of the position within the company._

Most employers base their salary offer on the first two value considerations – your salary history and the salary history of the position within the company. Your job should be to convince the employer that he or she also needs to include the third and fourth value considerations – the going market rate for comparable positions and your projected value to the organization. In other words, you want to be paid what you are really worth. You need to provide **supports** for justifying a salary figure that may not be initially acceptable to the employer.

Focus on Compensation Versus Salary

Chances are you will be asked about your salary history sometime during the interview process. When this occurs, you need to be prepared with an answer that accurately reflects your compensation history. While there are many ways to answer this question (see our discussion in Chapter 6), with narrow to exaggerated figures, you need documentation that reflects your honesty rather than your stupidity or deceptiveness. If, for example, you only include your gross salary figure ($50,000 a year), you will not accurately communicate your true value, which should also include any bonuses and commissions as well as the total value of your benefits and perks which could add up to another $35,000. Although you should primarily focus on valuing your gross salary, bonuses, and commissions, you also need to communicate your total worth – one of our "big pictures" – by documenting the value of your complete compensation package.

Know Your Comparable Worth

What do others make in comparable positions? Are you making more or less than the norm? Is the employer offering below or above the going rate for this position in today's job market? If the offer is below the norm, why is this the case? Is there something about this company you should know before investing your time and talent? Do they consistently reward employees below the norm?

Knowing what you are really worth in comparison with others in today's job market may be your strongest case for negotiating a higher salary figure than an employer initially offers. If you do your research on salary comparables, as indicated above, few employers will argue for giving you a salary lower than the competition. If they do, you may want to seriously reconsider your future with this company. Despite wishful thinking, the compensation situation will most likely not get better in the future. A company that pays below the norm will have to attract itself to you for other reasons, such as a perfect "fit," a wonderful place to work, a bright future, a very talented and collegial staff, or a great place to get invaluable experience.

Communicate Your Future Value

Hopefully, every step in the job search has been organized to clearly communicate your qualifications to employers. As we noted in previous chapters, the best way to do this is to focus on your **pattern of accomplishments**. Let employers know you are someone who will produce **results** for them in the future. Indeed, you're a problem-solver who will **add value** to their company by producing **benefits**. While your salary history and knowledge of salary comparables will strengthen your negotiating position, it's your **perceived future value** that will be most important in determining the final shape of your compensation package. For in the end, that's what the whole job search process is about – clearly communicating your qualifications to employers who, in turn, will offer you top dollar for your talent! Let them know you are the person who will quickly solve their problems and thus more than justify your salary "requirements."

5

Deal Effectively With Compensation Issues

KNOWING WHAT TO SAY and when to say it during a job interview can translate into thousands of dollars in additional income. Unfortunately, many job seekers make four critical errors when interviewing that may result in receiving a lower salary offer than might otherwise be the case:

1. Fail to prepare for the salary question.
2. Prematurely talk about salary.
3. Focus only on the gross salary figure.
4. Quickly accept the first offer given.

If you understand salary preparation, timing, and the whole compensation package, you should do well during both the interview and the salary negotiation session.

Turn Interviews Into Job Offers

In today's job market, you will probably go through multiple interviews with a single employer before being offered the job. In fact, some of our clients have returned for five or more interviews before receiving a job offer and negotiating a compensation package.

While many employers prefer talking about compensation before extending a job offer, it is not to your advantage to be drawn into such a discussion before receiving a job offer. In other words, the employer prefers these four steps of the interview:

1	2	3	4
interview –	salary discussion –	job offer –	salary negotiations

On the other hand, it will be to your advantage to focus on directing the interview along this progression of steps:

1	2	3	4
interview –	job offer –	salary discussion –	salary negotiations

Reversing the order of Steps #2 and #3 is the difference between giving the employer the advantage versus giving yourself the advantage in Step #4. As soon as you start discussing salary during the interview, the chances are you will lose the advantage when it comes time to negotiate the details of your compensation. When it's time to talk about money with employers, the old poker game analogy applies to the job interview:

> "He who reveals his hand first (signals his intention) tends to lose the advantage!"

Your goal should be to get the employer to signal his or her intention first so that you will be in a more advantageous position to negotiate a competitive compensation package. Knowing what the employer has in mind for compensation provides you with an important baseline from which to develop a negotiating range.

Postpone the Inevitable

Since employers try to quickly screen candidates into and out of consideration, they may raise some form of these salary questions at any time during the first, second, or third interview(s):

1. What do you currently make? (the salary history question)
2. What are your salary requirements?
3. What are you looking for in terms of compensation?
4. What would it take to bring you on board?

When and how you respond to these questions can make a significant difference in whether you will be invited to additional interviews. Your answers may also affect the shape of your compensation package.

There's a right time and a wrong time to put important things off to another time. In fact, timing is everything, and much more, in the job interview. When it comes to salary issues, **prepare, postpone, and redirect but don't procrastinate.** Our basic rule of thumb for responding to these questions is to delay a direct response until **after** you have received a job offer. Even in a third or fourth interview, you cannot let your guard down. You are on stage being evaluated. The more you can impress upon a potential employer that you are the right person for the job, the stronger will be your case when it comes time to value you in terms of a compensation package. Be very careful when asked this question:

> *Our basic rule of thumb for responding to the salary question is to delay a direct response until after you have received a job offer.*

"What do you currently make?"

This is not one of those idle, small talk questions. Indeed, this may be the first big minefield you step into during the interview. A direct answer to this salary history question can have major implications for both the outcome of the interview and the shape of your future compensation package. It's best to respond to this question by using one of these two approaches to postponing the question or redirecting the discussion:

Postpone: "I would be happy to discuss my salary history and requirements after we've had a chance to talk more about the position and how I might best contribute to the company. From what I've heard thus far, I think this is something we can work out to our mutual benefit."

Stop/redirect: "Like most people, probably including yourself, my salary history is confidential. I will be more than happy to share this with you once I receive a job offer and we start discussing an appropriate compensation package for this position and my qualifications. What were you saying about . . . ?"

If, on the other hand, the question is about your dreams or expectations, rather than facts about your previous earnings, you will be asked some form of this question:

"What are your salary requirements?"

Again, postpone any discussion of compensation until after you have received a job offer – which should occur during the final job interview. In this case, you might respond by either postponing your answer or using the employer's question as an opener for getting initial salary information about the position or switching the job interview to a job offer and salary negotiation session. Any of these responses would be to your advantage:

Postpone/Redirect: "I really need to know more about the position before discussing salary. Could we discuss this later – after we've had a chance to learn more about each other? By the way, I wanted to share with you the story behind the $20,000 performance bonus I received last year. . . ."

"I assume you offer a competitive compensation package. Am I right? (Pause for affirmation and then continue). I think we need to learn more about each other before discussing salary. Can you tell me more about my responsibilities and with whom I would be working?"

If you are in the second or third interview and it looks like you may be offered the job, you may want to probe the interviewer for more information about the salary he or she may be willing to offer. You might respond to the same salary requirements question by turning it around as follows:

Learn more: "What do you normally pay someone in this position?"

"What would you normally pay someone with my qualifications?"

"What do you have in mind for this position? What salary range would we be talking about if I were offered the job?"

End interview: "I would prefer discussing salary at the time of an offer. I don't mean to be presumptuous, but are you offering me the job?"

Prepare for the Inevitable

Since you know you'll eventually need to deal with the compensation issue, it's to your advantage to prepare well in advance of even the first interview. In real estate, the watchwords are location, location, location. Similarly in the job search, the watchwords are **preparation, preparation, preparation**. While you may want to postpone facing the inevitable, because you're uncomfortable talking about money, you simply must address it early on in your job search. Do what many successful people have learned to do in ending procrastination – always start the day by doing the most difficult, distasteful, and anxiety-producing activity. After that everything else is relatively easy and enjoyable to accomplish! If you think of the job interview as a $50,000, $75,000, or $100,000+ prize you can win with only a few hours of Q&A, preparation takes on new meaning. Indeed, your preparation may be worth $10,000 an hour. If you become a savvy salary negotiator, your preparation may be worth an additional $5,000 an hour!

The best preparation for negotiating a top salary is to conduct an outstanding job interview in which you impress upon the employer that you are the best person for the job. Keep focused on communicating your accomplishments to the employer. You'll tell him or her what it is you will do for them in terms of expected outcomes. Those outcomes should be directly related to similar outcomes you produced for previous employers and which can be documented in terms of statistics and stories of benefits you produced for other employers. You also should prepare well for the critical post-interview and post-job offer meeting – the salary negotiation session. You do this by conducting research on salary comparables and calculating the value of all elements in your ideal compensation package as outlined in Chapters 3 and 4. If you do this, you should leave the salary negotiation session potentially a much richer person than when you entered.

> *Your interview preparation may be worth $10,000 an hour. If you become a savvy salary negotiator, your salary preparation may be worth an additional $5,000 an hour!*

Keep Focused on Your Goals

It's very easy to lose focus when conducting a job search because of the many distractions along what will become a very serendipitous route toward a new job. While you'll find numerous interesting jobs, companies, and individuals along the way, and you'll be tempted to deviate from your plans, few will ultimately appeal to your central values and goals. Always keep in mind your primary goal:

Find a job you do well and enjoy doing, one that is a perfect "fit" for your particular pattern of accomplishments.

Perhaps you need to write this goal down and occasionally read it aloud. For in the end, the best job is one that allows you to practice your passion, the one that constantly rekindles your enthusiasm for work, and the one you enjoy so much that you can't believe you actually get paid to have so much fun! While that may not be the best paying job, it will be the most rewarding job for you both personally and professionally.

6

Asking and Answering Salary Questions

UCCESSFUL JOB SEEKERS know how to both ask and answer questions intelligently. For employers, the quality of a candidate's questions and answers provide important cues to their on-the-job behavior.

While most job seekers spend a disproportionate amount of time preparing for anticipated interview questions, few prepare intelligent questions they should ask of the employer. Forgetting that the interview should be a two-way communication dialogue, in which both parties learn a great deal about each other in order to determine if a relationship is a good fit for both parties, even fewer job seekers are prepared to answer and ask salary-related questions. Ironically, in the one area that has the potential to pay off the most, they prepare the least and choke the most. At this point, many hungry job seekers appear overjoyed just to be offered the job and thus grab the first offer by saying *"That works for me! When do I start."*

Ads and Applications

As noted in Chapter 5, employers are interested in getting you to show your hand as early as possible in order to determine whether or not you meet their financial criteria for employment. While they may ask

65

you during the first interview *"What do you currently make?"* or *"What are your salary requirements?"*, they often ask these questions in ads, on application forms, or over the telephone as part of a pre-interview screening process. A typical classified ad includes one or both of these statements:

Include your salary history.

Include your salary requirements.

These are two different requests that may result in similar responses. The first statement requires factual information – what you actually make or have made in the past. The second statement asks for your expectations or wishful thinking – what you would like to be making or what you need to motivate you to move to this employer.

> *Requests for "salary history" or "salary expectations" have the same intention – screen you into or out of the hiring process based on financial criteria.*

Both of these salary requests have the same intention – screen you "in" or "out" of the hiring process based on financial criteria. Here's where you can self-immolate or play the game to your advantage. This is a tricky situation. If you simply don't want to waste your time interviewing for jobs that may be beneath your salary expectations, go ahead and provide this information. However, doing so is dangerous if you indeed get called for an interview. Now the employer knows what your hand looks like. He or she may decide to make your last salary or salary requirement their budgeted amount. In fact, some employers are known to ask these questions in order to gather salary information on the going rate for positions. A form of salary research, employers let candidates inform them what the market will bear in the compensation department. After reviewing 100 applications which indicate 100 salary histories or 100 salary expectations, they have a pretty good idea as to what the going rate will be in today's job market for their position. Why pay more? At the same time, one of your goals should be to get as much interview experience as possible. You really never know what might be a useful interview outcome – perhaps a good net-working contact. Turning down interviews because of salary concerns is a very narrow-minded way of approaching the job search. The more information, advice, and referrals you get from both referral and job interviews, the better off you will be in the long run.

As indicated in the previous chapter, we recommend responding to such salary information requests by delaying your response. If you are asked to put this information in a cover letter which would accompany your resume, you can use one or the following statements:

Salary history:	"My salary history is competitive for my level of responsibilities. I'm happy to share this confidential information with you at the appropriate time."
Salary requirements:	"My salary requirements will depend on learning more about the position and how I might best contribute to your company. For now I remain open to the salary question.

If you are completing an application form that requests similar salary information, fill in the appropriate sections as follows:

Salary history:	N/A
Salary requirements:	Open

In the first case, N/A means "Not Applicable." Remember our dialogue in Chapter 5 in response to the salary question *"What do you make?"* The response was "It's confidential information" until a job offer is made and salary negotiations begin. Alternatively, you might want to establish a salary range which you can later use as a basis for discussing salary. This is appropriate if an ad or application is definitive about revealing this information – the employer will only review applications that include salary data. Respond by doing the following:

Salary history: $80,000 - $100,000 + benefits

Salary requirements: $80,000 - $100,000 + benefits

Use the same strategies if you receive a telephone call from an interviewer who asks about your salary requirements. It's usually best to say "Open" or "Negotiable" depending on the nature of the position. Remember, both you and the employer need more information about each other before assigning dollars and cents to your future value to the company. Always try to position yourself so that discussions of money and other forms of compensation are reserved for the very last meeting – the salary negotiation session – which occurs **after** you receive a job offer.

Referral Interviews

Referral or informational interviews occur when you network for information, advice, and referrals by meeting with friends, acquaintances, and strangers in what should be an expanding job search network which you are deliberately enlarging through a well developed networking campaign. As detailed in our companion volume, *Haldane's Best Answers to Tough Interview Questions*, the referral interview is one of the most effective ways of finding the perfect job. It's through the referral interview process that you develop important contacts and learn a great deal about the most important aspects of jobs and the job market. In the referral interview, you are the interviewer. You ask questions in your quest to learn more about jobs and employers. And one of the most important set of questions to ask deals with compensation issues. You, in effect, use the referral interview to conduct important research on compensation. For example, you might ask the following salary-related questions during a referral interview:

One of the most important set of questions you should ask during a referral interview relates to compensation issues.

- What would be a reasonable salary range for someone in this position?

- Can you tell me about the types of benefits and perks that usually go with this type of position? What can one expect when it comes to issues such as stock options, health insurance, vacation time, and relocation expenses?

- How much wiggle room do most employers hiring at this level have when it comes to negotiating a compensation package?

- In what compensation areas do they seem to have the most flexibility?

- Assuming one is very productive, what could he expect to be making at the end of two years with the same company?

- How would you go about negotiating a compensation package with such employers? Any particular advice on how to best handle this issue?

If you ask similar compensation questions of 20 or more individuals with whom you conduct referral interviews, you'll receive a wealth of information, advice, and negotiation tips that will serve you well once you receive a job offer. If you are reluctant to talk about money, these questions will also build your confidence in addressing this key issue.

Headhunters and Favored Middlemen

Depending on your employment level, salary negotiations followed by written employment contracts are sometimes left to a third party, such as a headhunter or executive recruiter. This is often the case for high-level executives who deal directly with headhunters or recruiters rather than with employers. The good news is that many of these professionals understand the details of compensation and thus are highly motivated to see that you get the best compensation package possible. After all, many of them are paid a percentage of your compensation for having recruited you to the company.

But the bad news is that you may not understand all that is going on between the parties, and they may not have your best interests in mind. Remember, even though most headhunters and recruiters have a vested interest in seeing you get a high salary, at the same time, they primarily work for employers who eventually pay them for their work. Once you are placed, these employment middlemen will probably continue working for the same employer. Therefore, you are well advised to do three things in such a situation:

1. Become as knowledgeable as possible about compensation issues.

2. Keep in close contact with the negotiators by asking lots of questions and indicating exactly what you want.

3. Involve your own third party which may be your lawyer or some other knowledgeable and effective individual.

In the end, you need to stay in control of the compensation package – your talent in exchange for the employer's salary and benefits.

Interviews That Value Jobs

As we noted earlier, do not talk about compensation until you have been offered the job. Your focus during the interview should be on demonstrating your potential value to the employer and learning as much as possible about the job so you can value it properly. You do this by asking many value-oriented questions and listening very carefully to what the employer says about the job and company. You're looking for clues as to what this job is really worth, clues that the interviewer may give to you when you ask a series of questions relating to the position. The following questions, some of which are indirect compensation questions, should give you useful information on what the position is most likely worth:

- Could you please outline what you see as the major responsibilities for this position?

- How many people would I be responsible for supervising?

- What size budget would I be handling?

- How do you see this position growing over the next 24 months? What additional responsibilities might be assigned to this position?

- You mentioned an annual performance review. Could you elaborate on how this operates as well as how it relates to compensation?

- How stressful is this job?

- What's the normal annual percentage salary increase employees expect in this company?

- What are the five major things most people really enjoy about working here? (see if compensation enters into the answer to this indirect question)

- How does this position relate to the one below it and the one above it?

- Do you feel this is one of the more attractive positions within the company? Why would someone within the company want this job?

- What happened to the last two people who held this job? Why did they leave? What are they doing now? Would it be okay if I spoke with them about the position?

- Ideally, what type of person would do well in this position?

- What motivates people to do a good job here?

Even if you are under intense pressure to talk about money earlier in the pre-interview screening process or during the initial interviews, resist the temptation to reveal your hand. The tendency on the part of both the interviewer and the interviewee is to prematurely ask the "how much" question – how much do you want (employer) and how much are you willing to pay (interviewee) – in order to gain an advantage in the upcoming negotiation process. Whoever answers this question first will probably be at a disadvantage when it comes to negotiating the final offer. Your answer may even knock you out of consideration for another round of interviews.

Whoever answers the "how much" question first will probably be at a disadvantage when it comes to negotiating the final offer.

Assuming you have been successful in delaying the salary question until you've received a job offer, now it's time to deal with the realities of compensation. You have a job offer which means the final step in the hiring process is to finalize your compensation package and get you moved into the company. At this stage, the employer will probably ask the same question he or she has been unsuccessful in trying to get you to answer:

"So, what are your salary requirements?"

As will become apparent in Chapter 7, it's still to your advantage to not answer this question with a specific salary figure. Instead, pause, think about it, and then get ready to ask some key compensation questions of the employer. If you have followed our advice so far, you should be very well prepared to talk money to power and walk away with a compensation package that truly reflects your worth to the employer.

7

Negotiate a Winning Compensation Package

ONCE YOU'VE RECEIVED a job offer, it's time to negotiate the compensation package. How you approach this situation will largely determine the outcome as well as cement your relationship with the employer. Using a few of our salary negotiation tips, you should be able to reach a mutually satisfactory agreement that reflects your value and professionalism as well as confirms to the employer that he or she made the right hiring decision – they really like you. Best of all, you may be able to negotiate a compensation package that is 10 to 20 percent higher than what the employer initially offered.

Six Essential Negotiation Rules

Attitudes and relationships are everything in today's workplace. You're not being hired to just do a job. You're being hired to work with others – develop and maintain relationships – in order to achieve company goals. How you negotiate your salary will affect your relationship, both positive and negative, with the employer. Your attitude and behavior will show as you get into negotiating the details of the compensation package. This is not the time to be confrontational, obnoxious, disingenuous, or quick to make decisions.

How you negotiate your salary will affect your relationship with the employer.

You are well advised not to approach salary negotiations from an adversarial perspective. After all, this will probably be your new employer and professional family. As you approach the salary negotiation session, keep these six rules in mind:

1. Don't be in a rush to accept the first offer – it's usually the employer's first and lowest offer.

2. Negotiate from a position of professional strength – valuable benefits or outcomes you'll produce for the company – rather than from a position of personal need or greed – things you want for yourself.

3. Be inclusive and employer-centered by referring to "we" rather than the more self-centered "I."

4. Remain positive and enthusiastic, as well as incorporate a win-win perspective, when negotiating elements within the compensation package.

5. Don't play deceptive games, such as lying about your salary history or stating you have an offer pending from another employer when in fact you do not.

6. Use time and silence to your advantage.

Attitude, perspective, honesty, timing, and enthusiasm are very important when negotiating salary. Remember, the employer has already recognized you as an important asset to the company by offering you the job – you've been invited to join the team. Don't disappoint him or her by getting off on the wrong foot by playing a competitive game of hardball. As you negotiate the compensation package, let the employer know that "we" are working together – win-

win – to reach a mutually satisfactory agreement, one that will benefit both parties. Indeed, that's what good team members are supposed to do – help each other come up with workable solutions to challenges.

Negotiating Your Future

Once you enter the salary negotiation phase, keep in mind that you are literally negotiating your future with the employer. Whatever salary figure you settle on will most likely be the basis for determining raises with this employer, especially if raises are given as a percentage of one's base pay. Therefore, it is in your long-term interest to negotiate as high a base salary as possible. If, for example, everyone gets a five-percent across-the-board raise next year, a five percent raise for a $75,000 salary results in $750 in additional income over a five-percent raise for a $60,000 salary ($3,750 versus $3,000).

At the same time, you want to avoid the across-the-board salary raise trap that often determines future compensation in companies. Be sure to structure your compensation package so you will be rewarded in the future for your performance. Therefore, include discussions of performance bonuses, commissions, and incentivized pay elements when you focus on the structure of your compensation package.

Who Goes First

People who are not used to talking about other people's money tend to feel uncomfortable when it comes time to negotiate salary. Wishing it were quickly over, they do one or two things that nervous people often do that works to their disadvantage:

1. Immediately accept the first offer with little or no discussion – literally make a 10-second decision that may be very costly in the long run.

2. Talk too much, listen too little, and think too narrowly about consequences, options, and alternatives.

Both behaviors will most likely result in a lower salary than what would have been forthcoming had the individual waited, listened, and thought things out over a period of time.

As we discussed earlier, he who shows his hand first usually loses the advantage when negotiating salary. Let's assume you are now in your third and hopefully final interview with an employer. Following our advice, you have not talked about compensation. Not only did you not raise questions about compensation, you deftly avoided the interviewer's questions about your compensation history or salary expectations by postponing the issue until you have received a job offer.

Once you receive a job offer, the job interview shifts to the salary negotiation stage. The employer may say something like this:

> "We believe there's a good match here. We would like to have you join our team and thus we're prepared to make you an offer. How does $60,000 sound?"

Ideally, the employer would love to hear you say *"Yes, that's acceptable. When do I start?"* But that's not good timing. You still have a ways to go before you finalize any offer. Whatever you do, don't appear anxious to accept this offer, even if it's higher than what you expected. Pause for 10 seconds, softly say out loud "$60,000?" as if you are mulling over this figure, and then pause 20 more seconds before reestablishing direct eye contact with the employer. Silence at this point may communicate to the employer that this is not what you had in mind. Get ready to shift the discussion from salary to compensation and from you to the position as you begin to further strengthen your negotiation position.

Don't appear anxious to accept the first offer, even if it's higher than what you expected.

In this case the employer has actually revealed his hand by stating the offer. In addition to having done your salary research, which indicates the salary range for comparable positions is $58,000 to $67,000, you now have information on how the employer has valued the position within his company as well as for you. Consider this figure to be his bottom or starting point from which you should be able to negotiate upwards. Combined with your research on salary ranges, his figure gives you a negotiation advantage. Alternatively, the employer may say the following:

"We would like to offer you the job, depending on reaching a salary agreement. What type of salary do you have in mind?"

This question may come in other forms, such as *"What are your salary expectations?"* or *"What will it take to bring you on board?"* Whatever the case, the employer wants you to throw out the first figure. If you do, he will probably have the advantage since he'll know where to start negotiating with you. Whatever you do, don't state a salary figure which you may come to later regret, especially when you learn that you settled for much less than what you could have received had you observed some basic rules of salary negotiations.

The best way to handle this question is to turn it around to get the employer to volunteer a salary figure. Respond to his question by asking this question:

"Based on what we've discussed, what would you offer someone with my qualifications?"

Another way of asking this question is:

"What do you consider to be a fair salary knowing what I'm likely to produce for you over the next 12 months?"

Some variety of this *"What's your offer?"* question should result in a salary figure. Once you know where the employer is coming from, you have a very important piece of information from which to negotiate your compensation package.

Thus far you should be in a very strong position to negotiate an attractive compensation package. You've followed the three basic rules for successfully negotiating a salary:

1. Avoided talking about compensation until after receiving a job offer.

2. Got the employer to first volunteer a salary figure.

3. Engaged the employer by listening, asking questions, and using silence to your advantage.

In other words, there tends to be an inverse relationship between time, listening, and silence when negotiating salary – the more you use of each, the more likely you will receive a higher offer than initially extended.

Focus on the Total Compensation Package

Keep in mind that a gross salary figure may only represent 60 percent of your total compensation with an employer. While you definitely want to negotiate as high a salary figure as possible, you also need to know what goes into the compensation package. Since you have not discussed compensation at this point, chances are you need more information on the company's compensation package. What's it really worth when assessed according to our checklist of compensation elements in Chapter 3? Is the initial $60,000 salary offer part of a $75,000, $90,000, or $100,000 compensation package? How does that compare to your research findings on comparable employers and positions?

Once the employer asks about your salary expectations or volunteers a specific salary figure, this is a good time to bring the larger compensation perspective into the picture. Respond by saying:

"Before we get into discussing salary, could you give me an overview of what would go into the compensation package here at XYZ Company? What, for example, do you offer in terms of bonuses, stock options, health benefits, time off, and perquisites? Do you have much flexibility with the various benefits? I would appreciate more information on what all comes with this job."

The employer's response should be a briefing on the major components that normally go into a compensation package related to the position you've been offered. This is a good time to sit back and become a very good listener as the whole compensation story unfolds. Take notes and ask questions that would better clarify the value of various benefits and perks. The longer you can get the employer to talk about compensation and see you taking notes and asking questions, the more likely your value will increase over time. Not only are you acquiring useful information on the compensation package, you're getting the employer to invest more of his time in you. Time is on your side. The longer you take in reaching an agreement, the more flexible should be the employer in negotiating various elements in the compensation package. At the same time, you need to understand the value of various benefits, especially if you want to trade certain benefits for cash, or if you can acquire value tax-free benefits in lieu of a higher salary. Above all, you need to know how much flexibility the employer has in offering benefits. Which benefits are negotiable and what are they worth? If you immediately jump into negotiating a gross salary figure, you may later learn your timing and picture were bad – you should have first understood the availability, value, and flexibility of various compensation elements before talking about money. While the gross salary figure is important, it needs to be weighed against other valuable compensation elements.

> *Time is on your side. The longer you take in reaching an agreement, the more flexible should be the employer in negotiating various elements in the compensation package.*

Stating Salary Figures and Ranges

Assuming you understand the total compensation picture, it's now time to negotiate a salary. If you've followed our advice so far, the employer should have been the first party to state a specific salary figure. For example, he might say the following:

"We're prepared to offer a $60,000 base salary."

Once you hear this, you need to do some quick calculating based upon your research of salary comparables. In this case, you know the going rate for comparable positions is $58,000 to $67,000. If this figure falls within your acceptable salary range, you have room to negotiate.

However, if the employer offers $50,000 and you know from your research that $58,000 to $67,000 is the going rate, your response might be quite different. In either case you want to focus on the salary range rather than a specific figure. Ranges provide negotiators with wiggle room. For job seekers, negotiating within an acceptable salary range can mean a 10- to 20-percent increase in compensation.

Let's first take the case where the offer falls below your acceptable salary range. In the case of the $50,000 offer, you might pause for 20 seconds, look somewhat puzzled, and then respond by saying this:

"That's interesting. I spent some time checking salary data for the same position in comparable companies within this region. Most companies pay from $58,000 to $67,000 for this position and include a signing bonus. Is there some reason why you would offer $50,000 when such a figure seems to be way below the norm, and especially given my proven track record for producing results?"

This comment should result in an interesting response on the part of the employer. He may say one of the following:

1. *"It's not in our budget to offer more at this time."* Sorry, but they can't afford you. It's time to literally part company.

2. *"Oh, I didn't know that was the going rate. Very interesting information. I'll check to see what we can do. We definitely want to be competitive in today's job market."* In the meantime, the discussion shifts to the benefits package. The base salary issue will be readdressed later, after the employer has had a chance to discuss this with his supervisor.

3. *"We do offer a signing bonus, an incentivized pay plan, and exceptional benefits which may be worth a lot more when you compare the total compensation package. Let's take a look at what else we can offer you and then work the figures."* The discussion now shifts to key elements in the compensation package. Be sure to focus on the potential value of direct compensation items, such as a signing bonus, performance bonuses,

stock options, and equity shares. Many other benefits, such as health insurance, come with the job, regardless of your performance.

The point here is that a salary offer below your acceptable range does not mean there is no room for negotiation. On the contrary, since the employer believes you are the right fit for the job, he may make every effort to put together an acceptable compensation package. At the same time, it may cost the employer several thousand dollars in additional recruitment and lost opportunity costs to find someone else to fill the position. It would be foolish to let you go without trying to at least negotiate an acceptable compensation package that benefits both parties. In the end, few employers want to develop a reputation for offering salaries below the norm. If they are to effectively compete for talent, they must be competitive in the compensation department.

> _Few employers want to develop a reputation for offering salaries below the norm. If they are to effectively compete for talent, they must be competitive in the compensation department._

By using incentivized compensation schemes, such as performance bonuses and commissions, they can quickly bring themselves into your acceptable salary range.

In most cases employers will extend a job offer with a specific salary figure:

> "Mary, I think we have a very good fit here. We would like to offer you the position. So let's talk about compensation. How does a base salary of $60,000 sound?"

If your research indicates a $58,000 to $67,000 range, you're in good shape for negotiating a higher salary as long as you think in terms of establishing a _range_ within which to negotiate. The best approach here is to take the $60,000 offer and put it at the very bottom of your range and respond by saying:

"I was thinking in terms of $60,000 to $67,000. Given my previous track record of accomplishments, is it possible to go $67,000?"

By putting the employer's figure within your range, you **establish common ground** from which to negotiate a higher figure. Using your range as the framework for discussing salary, both you and the employer have wiggle room. Chances are the employer will move to $62,000, you can counter with $66,000, and then both can agree on $64,000 or $65,000. If the employer is reluctant to move much in your direction, and you remain interested in the job, shift to benefits where you should be able to negotiate additional compensation.

Calculate Benefits and Perquisites

While most of your attention will focus on negotiating a base salary figure, do keep the big picture in mind, especially the value of the employer's benefits and perquisites as they relate to your particular needs. Before agreeing on a salary figure, be sure you understand the value of the total compensation package. If, for example, an employer offers tuition reimbursement, and furthering your education is important to you, this benefit could be worth thousands of dollars as well as advance your career development. If it's neither important nor do you have plans to use it, then this benefit has zero value to you. If you have special dental needs and the employer offers 100 percent dental care, this benefit could be worth thousands of dollars.

We strongly recommend familiarizing yourself with the checklist of benefits and perquisites outlined in Chapter 3. Circle the ones that are most important to you and then see to what extent the employer provides such compensation. In most cases, benefits and perquisites come with the job and are not subject to much negotiation. For example, if the employer offers numerous benefits and perquisites that you do not need or want, such as health insurance (you're covered on your spouse's policy), day care, or moving expenses, you may be able to trade some of these benefits for a higher initial salary. Health insurance, for example, may cost the employer $5,000 to $10,000 a year, depending on your age and benefits included in the plan.

It's important that you choose your battles carefully. You don't want to focus narrowly on acquiring a $100 perquisite, such as a professional membership or a cell phone, when you could be focused on increasing your annual compensation by $10,000 by negotiating several other items such as a $3,000 signing bonus, $4,000 salary increase, $2,000 in moving expenses, and $1,000 in additional personal leave time. In general, the following items on our checklist (Chapter 3) of compensation options are most open to negotiation:

> _Choose your battles carefully. Don't focus narrowly on acquiring a $100 perquisite when you should be focused on increasing your compensation by $10,000._

- Basic Compensation Issues
- Vacation and Time Issues
- Perquisites
- Relocation Expenses
- Home Office Options
- Severance Packages (primarily for senior executives)

Health benefits and retirement-oriented benefits tend to be standard – they come with the job and are offered equally to all employees at similar professional levels.

Once you know the value of the employer's benefits and perquisites, you should have the total picture from which to better focus on negotiating a salary figure. If, for example, you determine this employer's benefits are worth $20,000 to you but the benefits you receive from your current employer are worth $30,000, you should calculate this $10,000 difference when negotiating your salary. When the employer offers you $60,000, you should point out to him that your current benefits are worth $10,000 more than you'll be receiving with his company. Knowing this, the employer may try to adjust both the benefits package and the salary figure.

Responding to an Offer

It's very important how you respond to the employer when dealing with compensation issues. Remember, compensation is often a personal and emotional issue for both the candidate and employer. For the candidate, an employer's offer may be viewed as a personal statement of your value in the eyes of the employer. If it's a low offer, you may feel insulted and respond accordingly – *"How much did you say? That's really low!"* The same holds true for the employer. If he offers you a salary figure which he feels is fair and you counter with a much higher figure, as well as try to negotiate a list of benefits and perquisites, he may feel you are more trouble than you are worth, rather than more worth than you are trouble! Indeed, you may be viewed as a potentially contentious individual who is likely to nickle-and-dime the employer to death. From the employer's perspective, this is not a good sign for developing a productive relationship. If the candidate has learned anything from the interviews, there's much more to working here than salary, benefits, and perquisites. This is a great place to work and develop professionally! Chances are you will always be looking for another benefit or try to gain some monetary advantage from this employer. A savvy employer will immediately read the signs and may quickly draw a line in the sand – this is it; take it or leave it. This salary negotiation session may confirm his worst fears about hiring you – you may not be a good fit after all, especially as you began playing hardball with the employer.

Our point is that it's extremely important how you manage the salary negotiation session. You are developing a professional relationship of mutual respect. Again, choose your battles very carefully because they could backfire on you. Yes, money is important, but as employers and employees rightfully point out from time to time, there is much more to a job than just compensation. The best rewards are usually found in the nature of the work and people you work with. Is it a challenging job you'll really love?

Time and again employers draw a similar conclusion that is well worth remembering:

How you negotiate your salary will set the tone for your future relationship with the employer.

Negotiate like a professional who views this as an important win-win relationship, and you'll be off to a good start. Negotiate from a perspective of need and greed, where your attitude and motivations will be revealed, and you'll most likely be off to a rocky start. Unless you can convince him otherwise, the employer may soon conclude he probably made a hiring mistake.

Use Timing and Silence to Your Advantage

Many of our clients have found silence to be one of their best friends when negotiating salary. Silence often makes people nervous, especially when dealing with important issues. The tendency is for someone to intervene with talk when seemingly unnatural silence occurs. In this situation, you want to time your silence so it triggers talk on the part of the employer. Here's what often occurs with our clients when negotiating salary. The employer states a salary figure:

Employer: "How does $60,000 sound?" (*Wants to get this over quickly by offering an above average salary.*)

Candidate: "$60,000?" (*Clarifies the amount so there's no misunderstanding.*)

Employer: "Yes." (*Not sure how he's taking it. Expected him to accept this nice offer.*)

Candidate: . . . . . (*Says nothing as he counts to 30 – creating the 30-second pause. To the anxious employer, the candidate appears to be thinking over the offer.*)

Employer: "Let me do this. I think I can go $62,500. While this is more than what's budgeted, I feel comfortable with what you will be bringing to this job to justify this amount." (*Wishes to break the silence, assuming the candidate is about to reject the offer. This statement should keep everything moving in a positive direction.*)

Candidate: "$62,500?" (*Again clarifies the amount.*)

Employer: "Yes, $62,500. I think that's very good for this job. It represents a 10 percent increase for the position." (*Appears upbeat since he just gave the candidate a nice four percent raise without even being asked.*)

Candidate: (*Repeats the silent pause. Appears to be seriously considering this new offer.*)

Employer: "You've not said much. What's on your mind? Do you have any questions? Let's talk about this." (*Breaks the silence again since he feels this may not be going well. Need to once again take the high road.*)

Candidate: "Yes. I know the salary range for comparable positions is $60,000 to $67,000. I was thinking closer to the mid to high $60's, since I have a proven track record that I'll bring to this position. I know this is a perfect job for my interests and talents. I can be flexible. But I'm thinking closer to $67,000. Is that possible?" (*Moves his figure to the high end of the range. Still appears interested as well as communicates his flexibility and cooperation. States his salary range as a "research fact" and then proceeds to put himself at the top of the range, restates his potential value, and raises the "Is it possible?" question. He knows many things are possible when it comes to negotiating salary.*)

Employer: "That's going to be difficult to do. Keep in mind that we offer a terrific benefits package – 100 percent medical plan which includes dental, vision, and prescription; a matching 401(k); seven days of personal leave in addition to two

weeks of vacation which begins accruing immediately; and on-site childcare should you ever
need it." (*Again, tries to keep a positive tone by
shifting the focus to company benefits. Appears to be
giving something but actually has nothing new to offer
since all of these benefits come with the job.*)

Candidate: "Yes, you do have a nice benefits package which
I appreciate. But let's talk a moment about my
contributions to your bottom line. As I
mentioned during the interview, in my last two
jobs I was able to reduce costs by 15% within
the first year as well as reduce turnover by 25
percent over a three-year period. I've always
been a team mem-
ber who focuses on
making significant
contributions to
the organization. I
would expect to do
the same for you."
(*Stresses his extra
value to the employer
in order to justify
being paid at the top
of the range. Presents
the rationale that
being hired is a good
return on investment
for the employer.*)

> ## Case in Point
>
> *"I had just finished teach-
> ing a client how to do the
> "silence technique" of ne-
> gotiating (30 seconds of
> silence) when he was in-
> vited in for an interview.
> They offered him $90,000
> and he said they all sat
> there quietly, not saying a
> word, for 2½ minutes!
> Then the interviewer said
> 'how about $100,000?'"*

Employer: "That's what impressed us about your background. We would hope you would do the same
here." (*Confirms the rationale. At this point the
dynamics of the situation are slowly shifting in the
direction of the candidate who addresses the
employer's hot button issues – saving money, reducing
turnover, and improving morale. All of these issues*

have value that far exceed the candidate's salary
request.)

Candidate: "Again, I can be flexible. Is it possible to go
$66,000? (*Reaffirms his flexibility. Makes one last
attempt to get the best base salary possible. Knows
this may be difficult but wants to confirm to the
employer what he sees as his true value for the company.*)

Employer: "I'm already over budget on this position. Let's
do this. I can make a strong case for $64,500,
but that's the best I can do for this position.
Could we work with this?" (*Gives more in the
hope of bringing this to closure. Wants to appear
supportive, recognize the candidate's value, and
develop a win-win relationship. Above all, he really
needs to hire this person precisely because of the strong
track record of bottom line performance.*)

Candidate: "I understand your situation. Perhaps we could
explore some incentive options that would
make up the difference." (*Knows when it's time to
move on to other compensation alternatives. There is
nothing to be gained, except ill feelings and a potential
negative relationship, by playing hardball and
continuing to push on the base salary. Offers a real
win-win compensation alternative that's hard to
refuse.*)

Employer: "What are you thinking about?" (*Always open to
new ideas that will keep the momentum going and
would bring closure to the deal.*)

Candidate: "I understand I'll be supervising eight people
with an operating budget of $500,000. As I
indicated earlier, I don't see a need to increase
personnel. In fact, we should be able to improve

productivity considerably if we put into place the ISTP system I used successfully in my current job. I see us reducing costs by at least 15 percent during the first 12 months. Could we do this? I would receive a $500 bonus for each quarter I reduce costs by four percent. At the end of the first year, we can readdress my base salary as well as explore other incentive pay arrangements." (*Presents a win-win option that is hard to refuse – he only gets paid a bonus for performance that affects the employer's bottom line.*)

Employer: "We can make that work. That's a good idea. Then, do we have a deal?" (*Impressed with the candidate's proposal which will actually benefit the company more than the candidate. We're making the right decision in hiring this talented person. It looks like we have an agreement.*)

Candidate: "Thanks. I appreciate that. We're almost there. One other issue I need to address. You're offering two weeks annual vacation, and I know I immediately begin accruing vacation days at the end of the first month. But for the last five years I've become accustomed to three weeks annual leave. It's really important to me and my family since we always spend three weeks together on a major trip each year. Is it possible to include an extra three days at the end of my first year and then go to three weeks vacation next year?" (*Knows he is near the end and has exhausted most of the employer's compensation options. This last one is important to him and is something many employers work with, especially knowing it is a significant family issue.*)

Employer: "I need to talk to some people about this, but I think we can work it out. So, do we have a deal,

assuming we can extend your vacation time?"
(*Can always find some flexibility with vacation days.
This should be it. Wrap this up and finalize the hire.
Asks a question to get an affirmative response.*)

Candidate: "Great. I'm really looking forward to working
with you and the people I've met thus far. This
is my type of company. One final note. Could
you summarize what we've agreed upon and
send me a copy for my reference? I took some
notes, but I want to make sure we both understand what we agreed to." (*Reaffirms his positive
feelings toward the employer. Knows it's important to
get non-standard compensation elements in writing so
there is no misunderstanding. Needs to closely examine the details of how the incentive bonus will operate.
Also, needs a written commitment on extending the
number of vacation days.*)

Employer: "Sure. I'll e-mail it to you within the next 48
hours. Or would you prefer I fax it to you?
Once you've had a chance to go over the sum-
mary and get back to me, I'll put it in a formal
letter of appointment which will function as an
employment agreement." (*Everything appears to
be on a positive and professional track.*)

Candidate: "E-mail is fine. I'll try to get back with you
within 24 hours so we can finalize our agree-
ment. Assuming everything is okay, when do
you want me to start?" (*Knows immediate feedback
is important. Needs to arrange for his transition to
this new company.*)

Employer: "I assume you need to give your current employer the standard two-weeks notice. Is that
correct? What about starting on Monday, the
18th?"

Candidate: "That works for me. There's a chance my current employer may only need me for another week, but I'll let you know." (*Has conducted a successful win-win negotiation session. He's happy, the employer is happy, and the future looks bright for both. Each has successfully met their goals. Both are off to developing a positive and productive professional relationship. Each can say this is an excellent fit. Now, it's on to the next stage – produce predictable results that reaffirm to the employer that this was an excellent hire.*)

Employer: "The sooner, the better. Just let me know when you'll be starting."

Negotiating sessions don't get much better than this for the job seeker. Focusing on one's strengths, using timing and silence, knowing what's really important, and being professional at all times result in structuring a compensation package that reflects the value of the candidate. In this case, he's walking away with a compensation package that is worth at least 15 percent more than what the employer was initially willing to offer. Most importantly of all, this type of low-key, non-confrontational negotiation begins building a positive relationship with the employer.

Take Time to Think It Over

While it would be nice to have the negotiation session result in a handshake followed by an employment contract, in many cases the candidate may want to do some serious thinking before accepting a position. You may want to do this for these five reasons:

1. The compensation package is not exactly what you want, but it's a very attractive job. Need to look at this more objectively – outside a stressful negotiation session.

2. The job has important implications for your family, such as travel and fewer vacation days. Need to discuss this with family members.

3. You're interviewing for another attractive job which may soon result in a job offer. Need to look at alternatives.

4. Not really sure if this job is the right one for you. Don't want to make a rash decision and mistake. Need some time to do some soul-searching.

5. Still have important issues, from responsibilities to compensation, that need to be resolved. A lengthier period of time and more silence may help resolve these issues.

It's very acceptable, indeed a common professional courtesy, for the employer to let you think over the offer. You might end your negotiation by posing some variation of these questions:

"This really sounds good. However, I need to discuss it with my family. Would it be okay if I got back with you in a couple of days? I'll give you a call by noon on Friday."

"I really feel this is a good fit, but I need to do some thinking about my future with this company. Could I get back with you by Friday? I'll give you a definite answer at that time."

"I know we'll work well together and I really like the people I'll be working with. In many respects, this may be a perfect fit. But this is somewhat complicated. You see, I have a final interview with another company tomorrow. It was scheduled for today but I moved it to tomorrow because of this meeting. In all fairness to everyone involved, including you, I need to speak with this other employer to make sure I'm making the right decision. I'll let you know by Friday about my decision. Is that okay?"

Forty-eight hours is an acceptable time frame for contemplating a job offer. Use this time wisely to consider the pros and cons of accepting the position. If you feel you need to readdress certain issues concerning the job, write them out and go over them with the employer. There may be certain issues you forgot to address during the salary negotiation session. But make sure you contact the employer in the expected time frame. He is probably anxiously awaiting your decision. During this waiting period, your value will probably increase with the employer. After all, if you reject the offer, he'll have to resume the recruitment process which may be both costly and frustrating. In other words, you may still have some wiggle room for negotiating your terms of employment.

When It's Not Right

Getting invited to job interviews and receiving job offers are the signs of a successful job search. However, a new job has important implications for you and others. It can change your life, your location, your financial status, your freedom, and your relationships with family and friends. This is serious business on the level of making a major purchase or even getting married. As many people quickly realize, each job often sets in motion a series of events and relationships that can have a profound impact on one's future, both good and bad. Therefore, make sure this is the right job for you. There's nothing worse than starting a job and then discovering within six weeks that you made a serious error. Like a bad marriage, it's something you might tolerate, but it's also something that can be miserable, day in and day out. If you have a gut sense that the job may not be right for you, chances are it probably isn't right.

While compensation is important, don't let it cloud other important job-related issues. If you only pursue a job for economic reasons, you may find you accepted the job for the wrong reasons. Be sure to seriously investigate the nature of the work and the people you will be working with. Is this an exciting place to work, one where you can fully use your talents and interact with talented and challenging co-workers?

When it's not right, you'll discover no amount of compensation can make you happy with your work. Recognize the signs early – during the first interview – and move on to other jobs that better fit your particular skills and motivational pattern. Focus on what's really important in your work – those things that make you want to do your very best.

Handling Alternative Offers

If you are faced with multiple job offers, you should be in a very strong position to negotiate an attractive compensation package. While we do not recommend playing one employer off on the other in a bidding war, informing an employer that you have other job offers can strengthen your negotiation position. The conversation might go something like this:

> "From what we've discussed thus far, I believe this would be a perfect fit for us. However, I've also received an offer from another company which is $10,000 higher than your offer. I prefer joining your team because of the cutting-edge work you're doing in wireless technology. While money is not my major concern, a $10,000 difference in salary is an important consideration for both me and my family. Is it possible to match the other offer in some way? For example, I'm open to working out an incentivized pay scheme, such as quarterly performance bonuses and commissions, that could move us in this direction. Could we talk about some other options?"

If an employer really sees your value and wants to hire you, chances are he will find a way to do so. Your job is to let him know exactly what your value is in today's job market. Informing him of an alternative offer helps establish your value for this employer.

Propose Renegotiation Options

If you are unable to reach agreement on compensation but you still feel the job is the right one for you, consider offering a renegotiation option. This is essentially a proposal for an early performance review tied to a salary increase. Let's say you expect a base salary of $65,000 but the employer can only go to $60,000. As a trade-off, you've proposed increasing benefits and receiving quarterly performance bonuses – a real win-win option. If neither of these options are acceptable to the employer, or if they do not add up to your extra $5,000 in compensation, you should consider a renegotiation option. Here, you propose to re-examine your salary request for $65,000 in light of your first six months on the job. Such a request puts the employer on notice that you are willing to accept the position as long as he is committed to readdressing your request at a later date. You're also making an important statement about your performance – you expect to produce a set of accomplishments to justify your requested salary. This is a win-win proposal that may be difficult for an employer to turn down. It also forces the employer to work with you in setting goals which will measure your accomplishments over the next six months.

Walking Out, Coming Back

Some of our clients, who have encountered difficult negotiation situations, have used hardball strategies successfully. In some cases, they knew their value and were unwilling to compromise. By holding the line and being redundant about their accomplishments and expected future performance, they were able to get what they wanted. In other cases, they stated what they wanted and literally walked out of the negotiation session on one or more occasions because the employer was not responsive. In many cases, they were called back with a positive response.

You need to decide how you want to play this game. Hardball tactics do work in certain situations and with some employers. Indeed, there is a time and place for everything.

Case in Point

"Tom obtained a referral to a company executive in a small traffic signal manufacturing company. The president was conservative, set in his ways, and did not want to pay much money – but he did need a controller. Tom established his price, refused to budge, walked out of negotiations twice, but is now controller and CFO of the organization."

Nice guys do sometimes finish last. Our advice: Know your audience and how you want to relate to it in both the short and long term. Know what risk you are willing to take.

Written Offers and Contracts

You should take notes throughout the salary negotiation session. Jot down pertinent information about the terms of employment. At the end of the session, before you get up to leave, summarize what you understand will be included in the compensation package and show it in outline form to the employer. Make sure both you and the employer understand the terms of employment, including specific elements in the compensation package. If you accept the position, be sure to ask the employer to put the offer in writing, which may be in the form of a letter of agreement. This document should spell out your duties and responsibilities as well as detail how you will be compensated. If your agreement includes incentivized pay, make sure it details exactly how your commissions or bonuses will work – how and when they will be paid, set up, and measured. For example, will you be paid at the end of each quarter or at the end of the year? Do you receive a flat bonus, such as $1,000, or a percentage of the sales from an income stream.

Ask the employer to e-mail or fax you a copy of this document for your review. Let him know you'll get back with him immediately. This document should serve as your employment contract.

8

Getting Raises and Promotions

ONCE YOU ACCEPT A POSITION, make sure you perform according to expectations. Your just reward for failing to do so will be dashed expectations followed by an unceremonious parting of company as the employer realizes he hired someone who demonstrated excellent job interview and salary negotiation skills but who was obviously short on work performance.

Your compensation package will most likely reflect a combination of your past salary history, salary precedent for the position, your current skill level, and your perceived future value to the company. If you interviewed well, you should have presented an excellent picture of performance which resulted in a higher than average compensation package. You created high expectations to match your generous salary.

Understand the Rules

The best salary you will likely negotiate with your new employer will probably be the one you just negotiated as you accepted the offer. Once employed, you may have less leverage in negotiating salary increases short of a major promotion which would move you into a higher compensation range. Assuming you asked lots of questions about the company prior to accepting a position, you should have a clear understanding of how your performance will be measured and rewarded in the future. Does the company, for example, conduct periodic performance appraisals which, in turn, are tied to salary increases based upon merit? Or does the company give everyone an annual across-the-board salary increase that basically reflects cost of living increases figured as a percentage of their base salary and then give bonuses based upon group or overall company performance? What's the likelihood of being promoted to a position that falls into a much higher salary range?

Don't be surprised to discover that your new employer often gives salary increases in the form of cost-of-living adjustments (COLAs). Such increases have little to do with performance and everything to do with keeping your salary and the value of the position even with inflation and competitive with the market. If, for example, you receive a four percent annual salary increase, chances are you received a cost-of-living adjustment. In fact, most employers prefer giving employees annual cost-of-living adjustments in order to avoid inflating the value of positions. A $50,000 position that increases to $52,000, with a four percent cost-of-living adjustment, remains the same position after adjusting its value for inflation. On the

> *A raise is something you earn for performance that goes beyond what is expected for the salary you currently earn. Employers prefer giving COLAs and bonuses in lieu of raises.*

other hand, more and more employers prefer giving bonuses in recognition of exceptional performance. After all, a raise is something you earn because your performance goes beyond what is expected for the salary you currently earn. In other words, you should get a raise because you exceeded expectations rather than merely met expectations. Indeed, exceptional performance adds extra value to the organization and thus is most appropriately rewarded with a bonus. Since your performance will vary, so too will your bonus. When tied to a performance appraisal, the bonus becomes a performance bonus.

While many bonuses are given at the end of the year or on an employee's anniversary date with the company, other bonuses may be given at different times during the year. Companies that carefully monitor performance may give bonuses on a quarterly or semi-annual basis. Again, based on your pre-employment inquiries, you should know how the employer evaluates performance and gives bonuses or other types of raises.

If you do not clearly understand how you will be rewarded in the future, it's never too late to meet with your employer to discuss future compensation. You need to ask these two questions:

"On what basis can I expect my salary to increase in the future?"

"How and when is performance normally measured and rewarded here?"

You need to clearly understand the rules for salary increases so you know how to play the game. If you assume hard work and productivity are rewarded with a substantial salary increase but then learn you receive the same cost-of-living adjustment as everyone else, you will be disappointed and your future performance may suffer accordingly.

You should expect raises based upon the following combination of calculations:

1. **Cost-of-living adjustment:** Reflects annual inflation rate and is often presented to employees as a "salary increase" when in fact it is an inflation adjustment.

2. **Company bonus:** Reflects the company's overall perfor- mance and may be given as a percentage of your base pay or as a flat dollar amount, such as $500, $1,000, or $5,000.

3. **Group bonus:** Awarded to the performance of particular work groups or teams or tied to particular group projects.

4. **Individual bonus:** Reflects individual efforts and contribu- tions.

Ideally, you want to regularly receive raises based upon a combination of (1) cost-of-living adjustments and (2) individual bonuses reflecting your achievements. From the perspective of employers, company and group bonuses are easy to administer as well as avoid hard choices in measuring individual performance. From your perspective, you want to be rewarded for your own efforts, which hopefully you are documenting on a day-to-day basis.

The Expanding Position and Promotion

And don't be surprised to discover the position you accepted today will not be the same position you're in 12 months from now, although the salary may remain the same. If you are as good as you say you are, chances are your duties and responsibilities will expand considerably as you take on the new job and increase its overall value. You many find, for example, that the $60,000 a year position you accepted 12 months ago has now expanded into an $80,000 a year position. As the position grows, so should your title and salary. When this happens, you need to consider the possibility of discussing a promotion with your boss. A promotion would give you a new title and put you into a new salary range which reflects your new value to the company. In preparation for such a meeting, you need to document your duties and responsibilities and compare them, in a classic "T" letter format, to the original duties and responsibilities assigned to the position and reflected in your current salary as outlined at the top of page 101. This "T" format clearly implies that the position has grown considerably under your care. It suggests that it may be time to talk about a promotion to another position or re-titling this position to more accurately reflect its increased value to the organization. You, of course, recommend that additional compensation should be assigned to this new position with its expanded duties and responsibilities.

As your position grows, so should your title and salary. When this happens, consider the possibility of discussing a promotion with your boss.

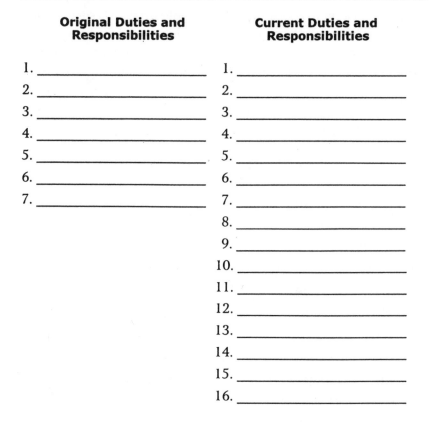

Original Duties and Responsibilities	Current Duties and Responsibilities
1. _____	1. _____
2. _____	2. _____
3. _____	3. _____
4. _____	4. _____
5. _____	5. _____
6. _____	6. _____
7. _____	7. _____
	8. _____
	9. _____
	10. _____
	11. _____
	12. _____
	13. _____
	14. _____
	15. _____
	16. _____

Performance Appraisals and Salary Reviews

Many companies conduct annual or semi-annual performance apprai-sals and/or salary reviews. If your company has such formalized procedures, be sure you understand the criteria for measuring your performance and how it relates to actual salary increases. Once you know the criteria, you should document your performance according to each criterion. After all, the employer should be keeping similar records of your performance. Your records should be more compre-hensive and detailed than those of the employer. If your company does not have such formalized procedures, it's incumbent upon you to document your accomplishments and present them in a special meeting with your employer where you focus on the position, your performance, and your future compensation – a raise and/or promo-tion.

Document Your Performance

One of the most important principles of job search success is to communicate your key accomplishments to employers so they can better understand your pattern of performance. You do this by "keeping book" on your achievements by documenting the who, what, when, where, and outcomes of your work. You should keep a diary of your achievements in which you document exactly what you did along with specific outcomes of your actions for the employer. This diary should become your "storybook of accomplishments" for documenting your performance. If you meet with your boss once a year to review your performance, this book should yield at least five major stories of specific accomplishments that benefited the employer's bottom line. Similar to telling stories in the job interview, these short 1-3 minute anecdotes emphasize your pattern of performance. Try to include as many statistics of your performance as possible, such as:

> *You should keep a "storybook of accomplishments" that documents the who, what, when, where, and outcomes of your work.*

"Saved $25,000 in direct advertising costs by developing an effective PR campaign that yielded more than $80,000 in free advertising."

"Reduced turnover in the department by 50 percent within the past six months."

"Reorganized scheduling procedure that reduced meeting time from 90 minutes to 15 minutes per week."

"Generated an additional $200,000 in sales in the past seven months through an innovative up-sale program developed through our Virginia Beach call centers."

"Negotiated three new contracts resulting in a 200-percent increase in revenue during the past nine months."

This type of documentation and resulting stories can present a power-ful picture of performance that begs the question – *"What kind of raise and/or bonus can I expect to receive this year?"* Without this documenta-tion, your employer will largely be in the driver's seat in determining your raise. And, as many employees are quick to note, their accom-plishments are often overlooked by bosses who do not document well what they actually do on a day-to-day basis. Therefore, it is incumbent upon you to take the initiative in presenting an accurate and positive picture of your contributions to the company. Be prepared to tell your employer your five major stories, which include lots of statistical supports or examples.

Documenting your accomplishments is also good for your long-term career health. There will come a time when you decide to move on to another employer. When that time comes, you should have a terrific inventory of accomplishments and compelling stories from which to communicate your qualifications to other employers. These accomplishments will become the building blocks of your resume, letters, and interviews.

Meet With the Boss

Whether or not you have a regularly scheduled meeting with your boss to discuss a raise, you should take the initiative to structure the agenda for such a meeting. Focus on developing a one-page "talking paper" which summarizes your agenda. It should:

1. Review your current work, including accomplishments.

2. Highlight your present compensation package.

3. Summarize research on comparable positions and compensation.

4. Propose changes to your job and compensation.

The emphasis here should be on **documentation** and **supports**. You want to document exactly what you do in your current position as well as emphasize your key accomplishments. At the same time, you provide supports in the form of comparative salary information for your proposed salary increase. If your current job description is no longer relevant to what you actually do, you may want to propose a promotion which might include a significant salary increase.

By presenting this one-page talking paper, you set the agenda which focuses on the position, you, your performance, and the employer's compensation package. As you bring these elements together, you make a reasoned case and compelling argument for a raise – you deserve it because you earned it through exceptional performance that exceeded expectations for the position. You're not talking about cost-of-living adjustments or being rewarded for group or company performance. You want to receive additional compensation for your specific contributions.

> *Don't be distracted by issues which divert attention from your contributions to the company.*

You also need to be prepared for objections to your proposed salary increase. These objections come in several forms:

1. It's more than what's budgeted.

2. You'll be making more than others here.

3. This will be a tough case to argue with my boss.

4. You're asking too much – we can't afford you.

5. Timing is bad because of the economy.

Each of these objections deserves a reasoned response that again emphasizes your value to the company. Your response also should empathize with your boss whose boss, in turn, may raise similar objections. Be firm about your focus – your accomplishments which benefit the company. Don't be distracted by other issues which divert attention from your contributions to the company. As a talented employee, you should be justly rewarded for your exceptional performance. If the company is unable to meet your salary expectations, be prepared to offer win-win options or walk. Win-win options might include a new incentivized pay scheme where you receive a performance bonus or commission for achieving certain goals over the next three, six, or 12 months. If, on the other hand, the company is unwilling to reward your performance with nothing more than a cost of living adjustment, perhaps you should seriously consider looking for another employer. While money is not the most important thing in a job, it does help you "keep score." If an employer is unwilling to celebrate your exceptional score, it's probably a good indication that you need to find a new score keeper who understands the value of keeping top talent.

Reach Agreement

Once you've reached agreement on changes in your compensation package, summarize your understanding of the agreement. Also ask that these changes be put in writing for your file in the form of either a letter or memo. This is also a good time to request a salary review within the next six months. Try to set up a procedure that focuses on reassessing your position and compensation in the not-too-distant future.

9

The Quick and Easy Salary Advisor:
33 Questions and Answers for Savvy Negotiators

MANY OF THE FOLLOWING questions have arisen in other forms in previous sections of this book. Other questions are best addressed in a simple Q&A format. This abbreviated Q&A section provides quick answers to some of the most important issues relating to salary negotiations.

The following questions are organized according to the major steps in organizing and implementing a job search. As we noted earlier, salary questions and issues can arise at any time during one's job search. Our compensation questions and answers address the various phases of a job search.

Whatever you do, make sure you are well prepared with the right answers to such questions. If you adopt our philosophy and approach – focus on your accomplishments and validate your value – you should become a savvy salary negotiator who knows what he/she's worth and communicates his/her value to employers who, in turn, provide an attractive compensation package. You'll negotiate the best terms possible in a very professional and positive manner.

Your Job Search

1. If I decide to change employers, what percentage salary increase should I expect with the new employer?

It depends on the job and your negotiation skills. The general rule of thumb is that it's probably not worth changing employers for anything less than a 15-percent salary increase. The costs of leaving one employer for another employer can be substantial – moving expenses, learning new systems, and extra work hours to get up to speed. Such costs are worth at least 10 to 15 percent of your current base salary. Anything above 15 percent should be considered a real salary increase. Keep in mind that your largest salary increase usually occurs when you change employers. This is the time when you have the greatest leverage for negotiating a substantial salary increase. Once on the job, you will most likely receive annual cost-of-living adjustments and/or bonuses. You may never again be in a similar strong position with this employer to command a salary increase.

2. As a career changer, will I have to take a salary cut in order to start a new career?

Maybe, maybe not. It depends on the particular career. If, for example, you have acquired additional education and skills to qualify for entering a new career field (used to be a $35,000 inventory manager who just completed an MBA at Stanford, where graduates start around $115,000 a year), you can expect to realize an immediate salary boost in your new career. If, on the other hand, you are moving into a new career field with little or no direct experience, you may need to take an initial salary cut to break into the field and acquire the necessary experience. Your previous salary in another career field should not be used as the basis for negotiating your new salary. In the long run, usually after three to five years in a new career field, most individuals more than make up for the initial salary cut they accepted in lieu of experience. They consider a lower salary to be an initial cost of breaking into the field.

3. I'm unhappy with my current salary. Should I start looking for a new job or would it be better to talk to my boss about a raise?

The grass is not always greener, nor more lucrative, on the other side. Deciding on whether to stay or leave really depends on how much you love your job and how well you communicate with your boss. If you really like what you're doing and the people you work with, see your employer about a well deserved raise or, better still, a promotion which might put you in a higher salary range. Do your research on salary comparables and make a compelling case that you deserve a salary increase because of your performance. Keep your salary discussions focused on the employer's bottom line – you are either saving him money or contributing to his profits by performing beyond the expectations for the position. Avoid any self-centered discussion about your financial needs. However, if your financial needs far exceed what you can expect to earn with your current employer or in your current career field, you may want to consider changing employers or careers. Many people work in career fields that do not generate much long-term earning power. They need to consider other career options. If and when you consider to change jobs or careers, see our companion volumes on making such changes – *I Want to Do Something Else, But I'm Not Sure What It Is* and *Change Your Job, Change Your Life* (Impact Publications, 2005)

4. I feel I'm worth a lot more than what my current paycheck reflects. What should I do?

Most people feel underpaid but few actually have data on what they should be paid. What, for example, do others make in similar positions within your community or region? Where does your salary rank compare to others' salaries – at the bottom, middle, or top? Be sure to do your research on salaries of comparable positions. Only then will you be in a strong position to talk about a salary raise with your current employer. You'll also have data that tells you if it's worth looking for a comparable job with another employer who would pay at least 15 percent more than what you are currently making.

5. When's the best time to address the salary issue?

The best time to address the issue with a prospective employer is after you have received a job offer. Avoid any discussion of salary before you have been interviewed and offered the job. Remember, you want to determine the value of the position as well as communicate your value to the employer **before** discussing compensation.

6. I usually accept whatever an employer offers. After all, isn't that what the job pays?

Most jobs outside government pay whatever the market will bear. The employer's initial offer is usually his lowest offer. Except for many pre-priced entry-level positions, most employers have some flexibility to negotiate compensation for most positions. Ironically, accepting the first offer on the spot may communicate an unprofessional message – you really need this job and will take whatever is offered. Accepting the first offer will probably result in the employer saying to himself, _"Boy, that was easy. Perhaps I offered too much. I wonder if he would have accepted something lower?"_ By negotiating, you build respect for yourself and increase your value in the eyes of the employer. You also set the stage for the next compensation stage – a salary raise.

Ads, Resumes, and Letters

7. What should I do if an ad says to include my salary history and/or salary requirements?

In either case, you need to avoid specifying figures that can screen you "in" or "out" of consideration or lock you into a low salary range. In the case of **salary history**, either ignore the question or state that your salary history is confidential but it is open for discussion should you be offered the position. As for **salary requirements**, you should respond by stating "open" or "competitive." The point is to avoid revealing your compensation hand. You need to learn more about the position as well as communicate your value to the potential employer before you start discussing compensation. If an ad clearly states that you must include your salary history or salary requirements as a condition for being considered for the position, include a range that summarizes your total compensation package: "a base salary in the $50s with benefits valued in the $30s." At the same time, this requirement should raise some serious questions in your mind about the employer's hiring mentality – he may be a tough negotiator who primarily focuses on compensation issues rather than on talent. Similar to the job seeker who initially asks the employer what he's paying for the job, an employer who indirectly asks you what you will accept demonstrates a rather shallow view of employees. Get ready to ask questions about how employees are normally rewarded in the company. You may be surprised at what you learn!

8. Is it appropriate to include salary information on my resume or in my cover letter?

No – never, ever, unless you want to suffer the negative consequences. Do so only if you want to be quickly screened into or out of the job interview. Revealing such salary information will inevitably put you at a disadvantage when it comes time to negotiate compensation because you already "showed your hand."

9. I may look over-qualified for a job I really want. From reading my resume, the employer may think my salary requirements will be too high. What should I do to make sure I won't be prematurely eliminated because of my background?

Make sure your resume follows the principles outlined in our companion volume, *Haldane's Best Resumes for Professionals* (Impact Publications). Your resume should emphasize your accomplishments – those things that resulted in benefits for previous employers – rather than your years of work history. Remember, employers want to hire your future performance, not reward you for your past work history. If you keep focused on what's really important to employers – benefits and outcomes –

you should have no problem getting the interview. It's during the interview that you may need to deal with a possible objection to your candidacy – that you may be overqualified. You can easily do this by focusing on what you believe is important to both you and the employer.

Networking

10. How do you learn about salaries when networking?

As outlined in our companion volumes, *Haldane's Best Answers to Tough Interview Questions* and *The Savvy Networker* (Impact Publications), your major networking activity should involve conducting referral or informational interviews with people who are very knowledgeable about your career field. In fact, one of the most important sets of questions you should be asking during referral interviews is about compensation. Assuming you are interviewing individuals who know your industry well, ask them if they know what the **salary range** is for the types of positions you are interested in pursuing. While it would be impolite to ask what they make, asking what others make is very acceptable. After interviewing 10 different people and asking them about salary ranges, you may discover the going rate for the position you are interested in is somewhere between $58,000 and $67,000. You also can confirm this information by contacting your professional association, which may conduct annual salary surveys of its members, and by surveying salary information on several websites (see the answer to Question #12 which lists relevant websites).

11. Is it appropriate to ask people about their salaries?

No, not unless you are operating in a foreign culture, especially in Asia, where asking personal questions about one's salary may be acceptable behavior. In most parts of North America, salary is a very personal matter which is seldom discussed with anyone outside your immediate family. What you make is usually considered to be your business and the business of your employer, who holds it to be confidential information. Asking your co-workers about their salaries can be grounds for dismissal. However, it's okay to ask about other people's salary from a research perspective. Rather than ask *"What do you make?"* or *"What does Emily make?",* ask this professional research question:

> "I'm in the process of doing research on salary ranges for individuals working in film editing. Do you know what the salary range would be for someone with five years experience in this field who works in a large production company in Los Angeles?"

> or

> "I wonder what film editors make in Los Angeles. Do you have any idea or do you know how I might find out?"

Always consider salary to be a private and secret matter when it's about you or the person you are talking with. But it's usually a lively and revealing subject when it's about other people working in organizations.

Research

12. What are the best resources for salary information?

Your single best resource for accurate salary information will be people who know current salaries in your industry, especially human resource professionals and representatives of professional associations who periodically conduct salary surveys. An active networking campaign should quickly tap into such rich salary resources. You also should consult the current annual edition of one of the key directories on salary ranges which is available in many libraries:

American Salaries and Wages Survey (The Thomson Group)

Several employment companies, such as Robert Half International (www.rhii.com) and Abbott, Langer, and Associates (www.abbott-langer.com), periodically publish wage surveys for selected occupations. Magazines, such as *Fortune* and *Inc.*, conduct salary surveys and publish them in special annual issues.

Several websites also provide useful salary information. The major ones worth visiting include:

www.salary.com
www.jobsmart.org
www.salarysource.com
www.wageweb.com

The Bureau of Labor Statistics (www.bls.gov) also has salary information. If you are a high-level executive earning in excess of $500,000 annually, you should check the compensation data available on the Securities and Exchange Commission's website: www.sec.gov.

Your local library also may have some useful resources, such as state employment information which often summarizes salary ranges for a variety of positions within your locale.

Interviews

13. When's the best time to raise the salary issue?

You should avoid raising questions about compensation. Let the employer take the initiative in asking about salary. And when he does, try to delay the discussion of salary until you have been offered the job.

14. What should I say if the employer asks me about my salary expectations early in the interview?

The employer may want to talk about your salary history or salary requirements during the first interview. However tempting, put this discussion off until you learn more about the position and have an opportunity to communicate your value to the employer. The longer you can put off this discussion, the more likely your value will increase in the eyes of the employer. If asked one of these questions, you can best respond by saying:

"If you don't mind, I would rather address that question later, after we've had a chance to learn more about each other. I'm sure we'll be able to deal with that issue when the time comes."

15. Tomorrow I'm going to my third interview with the same employer who has been pressuring me about my salary requirements. What should I do if he asks me again in this interview? I'm afraid I won't be offered the job unless I give him an definite answer.

If the employer persists in trying to get you to reveal your hand, you can stop the interview immediately by asking this pointed question:

"Am I to understand that you are offering me the job?"

The truth of the matter is that you simply don't have enough information about the job in order to value it in terms of compensation. By the time you get to the job offer, hopefully both you and the employer will have a good sense of what each of you are worth to the other.

Salary Negotiations

16. Who should go first in stating a salary figure?

Always try to get the employer to reveal his hand first. If he asks you the question *"What are your salary requirements?,"* turn this question around by asking:

"What would you normally pay someone with my qualifications?"

This question should get the employer to reveal his hand first. Alternatively, you might ask about the position:

"What does this position normally pay in your company?"

17. What should I say if the employer says "*We are prepared to offer you $60,000 plus benefits*" but I really want $65,000 plus benefits and perks?

Respond with a salary range that is close to his offer and is consistent with your comparable salary information. For example, you might say,

> "I checked on comparable salaries and discovered the range for this position is $60,000 to $68,000. Given my past performance, I was thinking more in the upper $60s. Is that possible here at XYZ company?"

Assuming anything is possible if the employer really wants you and your salary requirement seems reasonable compared to the competition, he may well move to $65,000 plus throw in a few perks.

18. Is it okay to play hardball when negotiating salary?

It depends on whom you are playing with. Some employers can be hard-nosed about compensation. In those cases, you may need to get tough and stand your ground, especially if you have a good case for justifying your compensation requirements. Part of being tough is being willing to walk away from the table and politely say "No."

> "No. I've given this a great deal of consideration and I know I'm worth $_____. I'm sorry but that, along with the benefits we've discussed, is what it will take to bring me on board. If you change your mind, please give me a call. Thanks again for the opportunity to interview for the position. I really think this would have been the perfect fit for both of us. But I understand and respect your position."

But make sure you know your audience. Playing hardball with some employers is a real turn-off and it can backfire on you. They may perceive you as being unreasonable and primarily oriented toward compensation. Whatever you do, make sure you put together a very reasoned case for your compensation requirements, complete with supports.

19. How much should I be willing to compromise?

Be willing to compromise on things that you feel are reasonable and still meet your compensation goals. But also be willing to hold the line when you know you are right. Don't compromise on things that you know will bother you in the future.

20. What should I do if I have an offer from another employer?

You are obviously in an enviable position. Use this offer to your advantage to let the employer know that you have an offer on the table from another employer. This information should hasten the employer's hiring decision by either offering you the job or letting you know he is no longer interested in you for the position. If you have two job offers, be sure to compare each, item for item, to see which one is the better of the two. If you decide the employer you would rather work for is the one with the lower offer, let him know your situation with the other employer. Chances are he will meet the other offer if he can.

21. Should I primarily focus on the base salary figure or on the benefits and perks?

You need to initially focus on the total compensation package by breaking it down into its component parts. Separate the base salary figure, which is taxable, from benefits and perks, most of which are nontaxable. While many benefits come with the job, other benefits may have special value to you, such as tuition reimbursement and on-site childcare. When you start negotiating the package, start with the base salary. Secure it first, and at the highest level possible, and then move on to the benefits and perks, many of which may be negotiable.

22. Which is easier to negotiate – salary or benefits?

Benefits and perks should be easier to negotiate since they often cost the employer the least to give away. Many simply come with the job. However, savvy salary negotiators also know there may be more to be gained by negotiating benefits and perks than focusing on base salary. After all, many benefits and perks are tax-free forms of compensation. In some cases, you may want to negotiate a lower base salary in exchange for some expensive perks, such as a car, laptop computer, or deferred compensation. Base salary may be the most difficult to negotiate because it tends to be inflationary. The higher the salary, the more it will cost the employer in the long run. At the same time, it's often easier to negotiate salaries at the $100,000+ executive level than at the $40,000 or below level. Salaries at the lower levels tend to be budgeted within narrow ranges. Salaries at the higher level are often more flexible because of the importance of such positions and the changing market conditions.

23. What should I do if the employer says my salary request is beyond what they have budgeted?

Become an empathetic listener who seeks common ground. Let him know you are aware of budgetary constraints. However, you've also done your research and know your value in today's market. If it's a position you really want but it doesn't pay exactly what you want, try to develop some alternatives. For example, propose an incentivized pay scheme in which you would receive X number of dollars in bonuses every six months if you reach certain goals which contribute to the company's bottom line. Also, ask for a salary review within six months to readdress your salary concerns. Finally, be willing to walk away on a very positive note:

> "I'm sorry we're unable to reach closure on compensation. I really appreciated the opportunity to meet with you and learn about your company. Please keep me in mind should this situation change."

24. I really don't need some of the benefits offered by my employer. Can I negotiate a cash equivalent in lieu of taking these benefits?

You can try. If, for example, you forego health insurance, you may save the employer somewhere between $5,000 and $10,000 in direct premium costs. If you don't use other benefits and perks, such as tuition reimbursement and childcare, which are available to all employees, you again save the employer a few thousand dollars. Indeed, you may discover you are literally leaving nearly $10,000 of unused benefits and perks on the table. Keep this figure in mind when you negotiate your base salary. You should remind the employer of your "savings" to him which you would like to have reflected in your base salary.

25. I've been offered a compensation package which is less than I expected? Should I accept the offer or walk away?

Have you explored other alternatives, such as incentivized pay schemes and a renegotiation option? Have you asked the employer why his offer appears lower than what you expected, especially since you have done your market research on what other companies pay? Finally, are your salary expectations realistic?

26. I'm in a dilemma – I really like this job but it pays less than I expected. What should I do?

Be tough. Be willing to compromise. Be ready to walk away. If they really want you, they will find a way to satisfy your compensation requirements. Indeed, they would be foolish to pass up the right talent for a few hundred or thousand dollars when their return on their investment (you) could be much higher.

27. How willing are most employers to negotiate salaries?

While many employers dislike the negotiation process, and they may make you think they have little room to maneuver, they also know it's part of the hiring game. Most employers have room to negotiate salary, benefits, and perks. You'll discover how much room they have to negotiate once you start the negotiation process according to the principles outlined in this book. In general, larger firms have greater leeway with salaries than very small ones and they are usually able to be more flexible with executive-level positions than with lower ones.

28. I really hate haggling and I tend to be very compliant when it comes to dealing with stressful situations, such as salary negotiations. Is there anything I can do to become more assertive about compensation?

Do your research, focus on your goals, and know what you are really worth in today's job market. Remember, it's your talent in exchange for the employer's money. Find a friend who can help you practice a salary negotiation session. The more you become familiar with possible questions and answers and the more solid information you have to share with the employer (your research results), the less stressful this experience should become.

Salary Raises and Promotions

29. When is the best time to see my boss about a raise?

The best time to address a raise with your current employer is when he is in a good mood to talk about money – just after he learned about the company's positive cashflow for the quarter. Also, try to avoid busy Mondays and Fridays or late in a stressful day. Avoid any of the following bad times: the boss just fired someone; the company is laying off five percent of its workforce; the earnings report is disappointing; the employer is going through a personal crisis, such as a divorce or a death in the family; or the office is trying to meet a tight deadline.

30. How much of a raise should I ask for?

If you've done your research on salary comparables and know what you are really worth in today's job market, you'll know exactly what to ask for. Be prepared to deal with several objections to your request, which usually have nothing to do with your contributions to the organization. Be a good listener but don't accept excuses that have nothing to do with your performance. Again, it's your talent in exchange for reasonable compensation. Keep focused on your value to the employer by giving examples of your recent accomplishments.

31. When should I talk about a promotion versus a raise?

You're more likely to receive a substantial on-the-job raise if you are promoted to a higher level position which has a higher level salary attached to it. You also should talk about a promotion when your job has expanded considerably from its original description. It may be time to talk about redesigning the job, re-titling the position, or a promotion to another position. In any case, you also should be talking about a substantial raise.

32. My current employer primarily gives across-the-board cost-of-living increases as raises. What's the best way to present my case for a real raise?

Keep a diary that documents your performance and enables you to develop a series of stories that illustrate your value to the employer. Show the employer exactly what it is you have been doing to justify a raise. Remember, salaries are to be earned, not given routinely for showing up and doing your job. Talk about those extras you have produced. These should be measurable outlines that have contributed to the bottom line. Don't just recite things you have done that are expected of the position. Show that you have exceeded expectations and that you should be rewarded accordingly with a raise or a bonus.

33. I asked for a raise but my boss turned me down. What should I do? Is it time to start looking for a new job?

Listen carefully how your employer responded to your request for a raise. If he is not planning to reward performance, consider taking your talent elsewhere. You should work for someone who appreciates your talent and rewards you accordingly.

Index

The Authors

OR MORE THAN TWO DECADES Ron and Caryl Krannich, Ph.Ds, have pursued a passion – assisting hundreds of thousands of individuals, from students, the unemployed, and ex-offenders to military personnel, international job seekers, and CEOs, in making critical job and career transitions. Focusing on key job search skills, career changes, and employment fields, their impressive body of work has helped shape career thinking and behavior both in the United States and abroad. Their sound advice has changed numerous lives, including their own!

Ron and Caryl are two of America's leading career and travel writers who have authored, co-authored, or ghost-written more than 70 books. A former Peace Corps Volunteer and Fulbright Scholar, Ron received his Ph.D. in Political Science from Northern Illinois University. Caryl received her Ph.D. in Speech Communication from Penn State University. Together they operate Development Concepts Incorporated, a training, consulting, and publishing firm in Virginia.

The Krannichs are both former university professors, high school teachers, management trainers, and consultants. As trainers and consultants, they have completed numerous projects on management, career development, local government, population planning, and rural development in the United States and abroad. Their career books focus on key job search skills, military and civilian career transitions, government and international careers, travel jobs, and nonprofit organizations, and include such classics as *High Impact Resumes and Letters*, *Interview for Success*, and *Change Your Job, Change Your Life*. Their books represent one of today's most comprehensive collections of career writing. With nearly 3 million copies in print, their publications are widely available in bookstores, libraries, and career centers. No strangers to the Internet world, they have written *America's Top Internet Job Sites* and *The Directory of Websites for International Jobs* and published several Internet recruitment and job search books. They also have developed career-related websites: www.impactpublications.com, www.winningthejob.com, www.contentfor careers.com, and www.veteransworld.com. Many of their career tips have appeared on such major websites as www.monster.com, www.careerbuild er.com, www.employmentguide.com, and www.campuscareercenter.com.

Ron and Caryl live a double life, with travel being their best kept *"do what you love"* career secret. Authors of over 20 travel-shopping guidebooks on various destinations around the world, they continue to pursue their international and travel interests through their innovative *Treasures and Pleasures of...Best of the Best* travel-shopping series and related websites: www.ishoparoundtheworld.com, www.contentfortravel.com, and www.tra vel-smarter.com. When not found at their home and business in Virginia, they are probably somewhere in Europe, Asia, Africa, the Middle East, the South Pacific, the Caribbean, or the Americas following their other passion – researching and writing about quality antiques, arts, crafts, jewelry, hotels, and restaurants as well as adhering to the career advice they give to others: *"Pursue a passion that enables you to do what you really love to do."*

As both career and travel experts, the Krannichs' work is frequently featured in major newspapers, magazines, and newsletters as well as on radio, television, and the Internet. Available for interviews, consultation, and presentations, they can be contacted as follows:

Ron and Caryl Krannich
krannich@impactpublications.com

Career Resources

THE FOLLOWING CAREER RESOURCES are available directly from Impact Publications. Full descriptions of each title, as well as 10+ downloadable catalogs and 40+ specialty flyers, can be found on Impact's website: www.impact publications.com. Complete the following form or list the titles, include shipping (see formula at the end), enclose payment, and send your order to:

IMPACT PUBLICATIONS
9104 Manassas Drive, Suite N
Manassas Park, VA 20111-5211 USA
1-800-361-1055 (orders only)
Tel. 703-361-7300 or Fax 703-335-9486
Email address: info@impactpublications.com
Quick & easy online ordering: www.impactpublications.com

Orders from individuals must be prepaid by check, money order, or major credit card. We accept telephone, fax, and email orders.

Qty.	TITLES	Price	TOTAL
Featured Title			
____	Salary Negotiation Tips for Professionals	$16.95	_____
Career Planning and Job Search			
____	5 Patterns of Extraordinary Careers	$17.95	_____
____	95 Mistakes Job Seekers Make & How to Avoid Them	$13.95	_____
____	101 Ways to Recession-Proof Your Career	$14.95	_____
____	America's Top Internet Job Sites	$19.95	_____
____	Change Your Job, Change Your Life	$21.95	_____

126

_____ Guide to Internet Job Searching $14.95 _____
_____ The Job Hunting Guide: Transitioning From
College to Career $14.95 _____
_____ Job Hunting Tips for People With Not-So-Hot
Backgrounds $17.95 _____
_____ Job Search Handbook for People With
Disabilities $17.95 _____
_____ No One Will Hire Me! $13.95 _____
_____ Quit Your Job and Grow Some Hair $15.95 _____
_____ Rites of Passage at $100,000 to $1 Million+ $29.95 _____
_____ Working Identity $26.95 _____

Assessment

_____ Discover the Best Jobs for You $15.95 _____
_____ Discover What You're Best At $14.00 _____
_____ Do What You Are $18.95 _____
_____ Finding Your Perfect Work $16.95 _____
_____ I Could Do Anything If Only I Know What
It Was $14.95 _____
_____ I Don't Know What I Want, But I Know
It's Not This $14.00 _____
_____ I Want to Do Something Else, But I'm
Not Sure What It Is $15.95 _____
_____ Now, Discover Your Strengths $27.00 _____
_____ What Should I Do With My Life? $14.95 _____
_____ What Type Am I? $14.95 _____
_____ What's Your Type of Career? $17.95 _____

Attitude and Motivation

_____ 100 Ways to Motivate Yourself $14.99 _____
_____ Attitude Is Everything $14.95 _____
_____ Change Your Attitude $15.99 _____
_____ Reinventing Yourself $18.99 _____

Inspiration and Empowerment

_____ The 8th Habit $26.00 _____
_____ 101 Secrets of Highly Effective Speakers $15.95 _____
_____ Do What You Love for the Rest of Your Life $24.95 _____
_____ Dream It Do It $16.95 _____
_____ Life Strategies $13.95 _____
_____ Practical Dreamer's Handbook $13.95 _____
_____ Self Matters $14.00 _____
_____ Seven Habits of Highly Effective People $15.00 _____
_____ Who Moved My Cheese? $19.95 _____

Resumes and Cover Letters

_____ 101 Quick Tips for a Dynamite Resume $13.95 _____
_____ 201 Dynamite Job Search Letters $19.95 _____

_____	Best Cover Letters for $100,000+ Jobs	$24.95	_____
_____	Best Resumes for $100,000+ Jobs	$24.95	_____
_____	Best Resumes for People Without a Four-Year Degree	$19.95	_____
_____	Best KeyWords for Resumes, Cover Letters, & Interviews	$17.95	_____
_____	Cover Letters for Dummies	$16.99	_____
_____	High Impact Resumes and Letters	$19.95	_____
_____	Military Resumes and Cover Letters	$21.95	_____
_____	Resumes for Dummies	$16.99	_____
_____	The Savvy Resume Writers	$10.95	_____

Dress, Image, and Etiquette

_____	Dressing Smart for Men	$16.95	_____
_____	Dressing Smart for Women	$16.95	_____
_____	Power Etiquette	$14.95	_____

Networking

_____	A Foot in the Door	$14.95	_____
_____	How to Work a Room	$14.00	_____
_____	Masters of Networking	$16.95	_____
_____	The Savvy Networker	$13.95	_____

Interviews

_____	101 Dynamite Questions to Ask At Your Job Interview	$13.95	_____
_____	The $100,000+ Job Interview	$19.95	_____
_____	Job Interview Tips for People With Not-So-Hot Backgrounds	$14.95	_____
_____	KeyWords to Nail Your Job Interview	$17.95	_____
_____	Interview for Success	$15.95	_____
_____	Job Interviews for Dummies	$16.99	_____
_____	Nail the Job Interview	$13.95	_____
_____	Savvy Interviewing: The Nonverbal Advantage	$12.95	_____

Salary Negotiations

_____	Dynamite Salary Negotiations	$15.95	_____
_____	Get a Raise in 7 Days	$14.95	_____

Directories

_____	Almanac of American Employers	$199.99	_____
_____	Associations USA	$75.00	_____
_____	Directory of Executive Recruiters	$49.95	_____
_____	Directory of Websites for International Jobs	$19.95	_____
_____	Headquarters USA	$190.00	_____
_____	Occupational Outlook Handbook	$16.90	_____
_____	O*NET Dictionary of Occupational Titles	$39.95	_____

____ Plunkett's Financial Services Industry Almanac $249.95 _____

Career Exploration and Alternatives

____	25 Jobs That Have It All	$14.95 _____
____	50 Cutting Edge Jobs	$15.95 _____
____	100 Great Jobs and How to Get Them	$17.95 _____
____	300 Best Jobs Without a Four-Year Degree	$16.95 _____
____	America's Top 100 Jobs for People Without a	
	Four-Year Degree	$19.95 _____
____	Best Jobs for the 21st Century	$19.95 _____
____	Cool Careers for Dummies	$19.99 _____

SUBTOTAL _____

Virginia residents add 5% sales tax _____

POSTAGE/HANDLING ($5 for first
product and 8% of SUBTOTAL) $5.00

8% of SUBTOTAL ------------------------------- _____

TOTAL ENCLOSED -------------------- _____

SHIP TO:

NAME _____

ADDRESS: _____

_____

_____

PAYMENT METHOD:

❑   I enclose check/money order for $ _____ made payable to
IMPACT PUBLICATIONS.

❑   Please charge $ _____ to my credit card:

    ❑ Visa   ❑ MasterCard   ❑ American Express   ❑ Discover

    Card # _____ Expiration date: _____/_____

    Signature _____

Keep in Touch . . .
On the Web!

www.impactpublications.com
www.ishoparoundtheworld.com
www.travel-smarter.com
www.winningthejob.com
www.veteransworld.com